OF LITTLE FAITH

FAITH

[A NOVEL]

CAROL HOENIG

STEEL CUT PRESS Ⓢ

GLENDALE, CALIFORNIA

OF LITTLE FAITH

ISBN-10: 1-93638-005-6
ISBN-13: 978-1-93638-005-3

LCCN: 2013941709

Cover and book design by Paul K. Austad (p.k.austad@gmail.com)

Cover photograph: *Ruins of 3rd Presbyterian Church, Trenton, N.J., burned July 4th, 1879 - from Robert N. Dennis collection of stereoscopic views.*

Other images from iStockphoto and Wikimedia Commons

Interior text was set in ARNO PRO; with titles in PRIVA

Printed in the United States of America

STEEL CUT PRESS
www.steelcutpress.com
P. O. Box 1497
Glendale CA 91209
ph | 818.801.0353

"Our only deadlines are those we impose on ourselves."

OF LITTLE FAITH

BY CAROL HOENIG

Compassion Cures More Sins than Condemnation

—HENRY WARD BEECHER

For Connie

You've shown me how sisters can become friends.

Acknowledgements

Writing is often a lonely pursuit, one that requires patience and perseverance. With that in mind, it is those who encourage and offer support that must be thanked; otherwise, it would be easier to keep one's work private and avoid disappointment. Anyone who has attempted to get published knows what I mean. Therefore, I realize I am risking omitting someone who deserves to be acknowledged on this page, but I will take the chance to thank the following people:

Thank you to Debbi Honorof, Brenda Janowitz, Ellen Meister and Saralee Rosenberg. Our lunches are always enlightening and enjoyable, your friendship cherished.

Thank you to Lori Ames for always keeping me laughing, not to mention busy!

And, how could I forget my Book & a Bottle book discussion group, all willing to read a close-to-final draft of this novel as one of our selections. I was bold to ask if they'd include it as one of our monthly picks, but they welcomed it and gave me helpful feedback. How fortunate I am to have you all in my life.

Then, of course, there is Mary Walker Baron and Steel Cut Press. Imagine my delight when Mary approached me about publishing *Of Little Faith;* my appreciation goes further for her support in seeing that it is given every chance to find an audience. Thank you, Mary. You are an amazing talented writer in your own right and I couldn't be more grateful.

Having a sister who always enjoyed my writings—from my earliest poems and all that followed—is a gift. Thank you, Connie, for the continued encouragement. I don't take it for granted.

Finally, I must thank Jason, Corrie and Natasha, all who were first-hand witnesses as the novel unfolded. While *Of Little Faith* was developing into a fully realized story, my children grew into delightful adults who I am thrilled to call "my friends."

And, to you, for taking time out of your busy life to spend it in "Sumner Territory," I thank you.

CHAPTER ONE

Laura

I've been away for awhile, but now I'm back and surrounded by the familiarity from my younger days. There is the same coffee table, now scratched with age. Up against the wall near the stairs is the stereo console with the built-in turntable, except the needle is broken. The brown couch I am sunk in is threadbare and faded. Yes, it's all familiar and so is the reminder that I don't belong here.

Even though I grew up in this house, I never considered it home. The once brightly painted walls are dingy, the plush carpet, worn down almost to the bare floor. Mom wasn't big on decorating. She concentrated more on preparing for her place in heaven. Beth, Eric and I were expected to do the same. Imagine being required to focus on a place of dubious existence during a time when we were celebrating a won war; a time when the pulsating, unique beat of rock and roll began to pour through the woodwork and into our hungry souls; a time when black and white televisions took up prominent space in the living rooms of our Long Island neighbors. A new world was opening up, one with a variety of mind-expanding ideas, ideas my mother believed were inspired by the devil himself.

But I am older now and young men are being drafted into another war, this one undeclared, and the music is filled with protest and anger. It's a time for questions.

I have Sunday's NEWSDAY scattered around me and the radio dial on a top forties station.

All the leaves are brown and the sky is grey ...
I've been for a walk on a winter's day ...

Dust motes drift in the sunlight streaming through the window and I want to be one of them, the tiniest of specks freer than I will ever actually be. And, normally I would feel relaxed in my jeans and oversized shirt—a shirt that had been my father's—but I am far from comfortable. Maybe it's because Sundays were never a jeans and sloppy shirt day. No, there were years of frilly dresses and patent leather shoes, and being forced to stay dressed that way throughout the Seventh Day set aside for rest and worship. I was a child. I had too much energy to rest, and what did I care about worship?

I turned the page of the newspaper from a photograph of two young boys, younger than me, burning their draft cards protesting the Vietnam mess. The following page has an article about the abortion rally in New York. Curiously, there was a sidebar advertisement of a young glowing mother holding her infant. The ad was for Gerber's Baby food. I was debating if the layout was intentional when I heard a car pull into the driveway. That would be Beth. I took a deep breath. One has to prepare for my sister who does piety the way some folks do drugs, and she overdoses on Sunday.

Stopped into a church i passed along the way …

Three car doors slammed shut. No surprise there.

I got down on my knees and pretend to pray …

The front door opened with Beth already in mid-sentence.

"—was one of your best sermons yet, Eric." She swept into the room, her hefty Bible cradled in her arms. My brother Eric held the door opened for Jenny.

I forced a smile, even as Beth marched over to the radio.

California drea—

She flipped the dial.

O, God, our help in ages past,

"Our hope in years to come…," Beth sang with the blaring notes from an organ.

I suppose the old hymns could soothe a restless soul, but not mine. They brought other memories I'd rather not recall. I rested the paper on my lap and watched Sunday's routine unfold. Eric, with Jenny in tow, strolled in and acknowledged me with a nod. Beth motioned for me to make room for them, before placing her Bible in its rightful spot on the rickety end table.

"Smells great," Eric said. "Roast beef?"

Beth nodded and stood over me, her hands placed akimbo on her thick waistline. "When did you check on it last?"

"Just before," I said. The answer didn't satisfy Beth and she took off into the kitchen.

Eric landed in the worn plaid armchair across from me. Jenny sank in the matching love seat, which immediately swallowed her.

"Eric!" Beth called from the kitchen. "Tell Laura how many came forward today."

I looked over at Eric, trying to express an interest, but he cleared his throat and said, "I'm sure you don't really care."

I shrugged. "You can tell me about it, if you want."

Jenny's long thin fingers twisted a strand of stringy brown hair. "Eric really inspires them."

"Well," Eric said, "I think half of them came up just to tell me again how sorry they were about Dad." He loosened his tie and tossed it on the arm of the chair. "That his shirt you're wearing?"

I touched the grey cotton button down and nodded.

"Everything'll be ready in a few minutes," Beth said, coming back into the living room. She plopped down next to me with a grunt. "Meanwhile, let's visit."

I knew what that meant. Beth had just come from Sunday service and was itching to let me know about the healing and praising that I missed.

I shifted to the edge of the couch, and said, "There is something I want to discuss with you. Actually, with ALL of you."

"You know," Beth said, "on the way home I was telling Eric ... and Jenny, of course, how sad it was that you missed today's service. Deacon Don shared the most inspirational verses."

"I'm sure," I said, "but I wanted—"

Up from the grave he arose ...

Beth joined in with the radio. "He arose! He arose!"

Eric cleared his throat, and said, "Laura, you had something to say?"

I sat up straighter and said, "Yeah."

"I know what it is," Jenny said, her eyes bright. "You sold your book!"

I smiled, but shook my head. "We're still waiting to hear from the publisher." It had been a couple of months ago when I gave my manuscript to Loren, my agent. I usually badger him to find out what's going on, but with Dad's recent death, Loren had been given a respite from me.

"What's the name of it again?" Jenny said.

"The Pink Goose."

"The Pink Goose!" Beth said, abandoning the song. "That doesn't sound right. Wouldn't it be better if it had more of a, well, a religious title?" She gazed at me; her blue eyes so much like our mother's—eyes that could stop you short if you let them. "I mean, wouldn't it be wonderful if it had a message for children? You could sell dozens at Christian bookstores and—"

"It does have a message, Beth, but more of a universal one."

"You mean worldly, don't you?"

"Uh," Eric said, "is it your job? You did tell them that your father died, right?"

"No, things are okay. I mean, they still give me a hard time being the only female reporter there and all, but they're still giving me stories to cover."

"That must be so exciting," Jenny said.

"Well, the potatoes won't mash themselves," Beth said, standing.

"But we haven't talked yet!" I called.

"Can't it wait?" she said. "The table needs to be set and the meat sliced."

Eric and Jenny got up and followed Beth. Being on Sumner territory meant I was to play by their rules. I still think of it as me by myself against them, even with Mom dead for close to four years. I got up and went about the task of setting the table while Good News Gospel Hour continued pumping out one hymn after the next. Mom used to keep it on all through Sunday dinner.

He walks with me and he talks with me ...

I went over to the radio and clicked it off.

After, I pushed through the swinging door to the kitchen. Beth was mashing a bowl of potatoes, the loose flesh of her arms jiggling, the whirring of the beaters drowning out any hope for conversation. Eric was busy slicing the meat while Jenny was filling the bread basket with rolls hot out of the oven.

Beth stopped the beaters and looked over at me. "Table set?"

I nodded and picked up the bowl of green beans, carrying them to the dining room. Soon, we were all sitting around the table, our heads bowed.

While Eric thanked God for everything from the blooming crocuses to the sustenance before us, I thought about the bottle of wine stuffed in one of the boxes from my recent, incomprehensible move. I even imagined skipping upstairs to the bedroom to retrieve it. A glass of Cabernet would have been extremely satisfying just then, but the simple act of uncorking Satan's brew would be enough to stir Beth's holy fire. The water already poured would have to suffice.

After Eric ended the prayer he reached for the platter of roast beef. Beth scooped out some potatoes and dropped them on to her plate. I attempted once again to bring up the topic that was on my mind, but Beth interjected, "I've been giving a lot of thought to this year's VBS theme."

So now we were supposed to talk about Vacation Bible School.

"What did you have in mind?" Eric said.

"I was thinking about teaching the young people how they should respect authority. Seeing all those war protesters on television everyday is setting a wrong example. And that would make a good sermon, too, Eric."

Jenny nodded in agreement.

With a mouthful of beef, Eric wasn't able to respond. Either that or he purposely chewed so that he would not have to. I scooped up some beans, letting them fall to my plate one by one while Beth went on about the ungodly hippies with their peace signs and free love. There was no stopping her until she mentioned the word "money."

"We just have to find a way to raise more in order to keep feeding the shut-ins," she said.

"I know what you mean," I said. "I have a friend who helps out at a rehab. She's always saying how strapped they are for money."

Beth studied me for a moment before saying, "I hardly think the two compare."

"What do you mean?" Eric said.

"Well, the people I'm talking about don't bring their problems on themselves." She punctuated her sentence by shoving a piece of beef into her mouth.

I rested my fork on my plate with a sigh and said, "Since you brought up the topic of money, I think it's time for us to go to the bank and get some advice about the house."

Everyone stopped chewing and stared at me.

"What do you mean," Beth said, *"about the house?"*

"Well, are we going to sell it or what?"

Beth played with her frizzy brown hair. "Heaven's, Laura, it's only been a couple of weeks since Dad died."

"I know, Beth, and I'm not trying to sound greedy, but I ... I could use the money. The Will specifically stated that we divvy out the profit from the house once it's sold."

"He didn't mean right away!"

"How do you know what he meant?" I said, wondering when Eric was going to insinuate himself into the conversation.

"How do *you?*" she said.

"I'm not sure why we would need to wait," I said. *Any time, Eric. Just jump right in.*

"Because it's really not necessary," Beth said. "You have your...your commune in the city and Eric has the parsonage."

"It's not a commune. Besides, I'm not going back," I said. I'd shared a loft in the Village with some friends, and over the years old ones moved out, some to marry, others drafted, while new ones moved in. Eventually, everyone had moved out, except for Stefanos and me. Funny how once the others were out of the way, it made more room for Stefanos to wander into my space, then I into his. Turned out we didn't bother searching for new tenants. Then after Dad died, I returned to Seabrook and found it difficult to make my way back.

Beth reached across the table and placed her hand on mine. "That's fine," she said. "You can stay here. There's no need to sell."

It was odd seeing her hand on mine. I averted my eyes. "I can't stay here."

"We've enjoyed you being around," Eric said. "Even if it was for something so sad."

"Thanks," I said, "but I can't."

"Why?" Beth said, her tone pleading. "Why don't you just give this a chance?"

I slipped my hand out from under hers. "A chance?" The wonder of it: the chance to be a family, to laugh together for no other reason than to laugh.

"I was thinking, if I sell my share of the house to you," I turned to Eric, "and you, I could use the money to buy my own place."

His plate scraped clean, Eric pushed away from the table. "We'd have to get a lawyer to figure it all out."

"Figure all what out?" Beth's voice was shrill, her eyes wide.

"The legalities."

"You're not serious, Eric. Selling Mom and Dad's house?"

"I need the money, Beth," I said. "We all do."

"Money!" she said. "All this talk about money!"

"You could use it for the shut-ins," I said. I wasn't trying to be amusing, but Jenny began to laugh, and then immediately stifled it with her napkin.

"And where would I live?" Beth said.

"You'll have options, Beth," Eric said. "This house is bigger than you need."

"But it's my home," she said, her expression stricken.

Unlike Eric and myself, Beth never lived anywhere else all her life, except for a few months when she went off to some retreat to get closer to God. It must've worked because when she came back she was always in her room praying. Then it struck me that she wouldn't have to move. All she'd have to do was buy out Eric's and my share. I made the suggestion.

She straightened her napkin. "That's just not possible. Not on my salary. After all, you're settled in, Laura. Why don't you just stay?"

Although my clothes were hanging in the closet and my toiletries were scattered all over the bathroom, I felt far from "settled in." I began to massage my forehead, to wish the sudden headache away. Barely above a whisper, I said, "I can't stay."

"But you could make it your home again," Beth said.

Again? I always thought a home should be a place for escape and safety, a place for comfort. I said, "What about Eric and Jenny? I'm sure they could use the money."

Eric and Jenny exchanged glances.

"I bet the bank could figure out your budget, Beth. Lots of teachers own their own houses. It's doable."

Beth jumped up from her chair. In one fast swoop, she gathered the plates and began scraping off any leftovers. "I suppose everyone's done," she said, her nostrils flaring.

"Don't be upset, Beth," Jenny said, barely above a whisper.

"I work hard to make a nice meal and this is the thanks I get." She dropped down the dishes and thumped over to the window, yanking the blinds open. "It's so hot in here, the oven going all morning." She tried to open the window, and when it wouldn't budge, she began banging on the sash.

Eric tossed his napkin on the pile of dirty dishes and looked mildly amused as he strode across the room and shoved the window open.

Beth sucked up some air, appearing to try to gather her senses, before lumbering back to the table, wringing her hands. "Okay then," she said, "why don't we have some dessert? I have chocolate cake and—"

"Chocolate cake's not going to change my mind, Beth," I said. "I want to discuss this."

"You know, leave it to you, Laura, to cause problems. Eric hasn't said a blessed word about selling the house, but then you have to pick now when we're having a wonderful dinner—"

"It was very good, Beth. And I don't mean to start trouble, but I can't go on like this. I just can't." I tried to remain calm and composed, but it was becoming more difficult as the conversation continued.

"Why?" she said. "Why can't you just live here with me? We *are* sisters, after all."

Jenny picked up the stack of dishes and headed to the kitchen; Jenny, the sister-in-law. Friends of Dad's who came to the wake thought we were sisters, the two of us five feet four with the same high cheek bones and similar straight hair, except mine was blonde while hers was brown. However, I always thought of Jenny as someone resigned to what life had to offer her. Me? I'm always ready for battle, my skin a veritable coat of armor. I don't know, though; because sometimes I feel I'm going to shatter, snap, crumble into myself.

"Beth," I said, getting up from the table, "it's a nice idea, but we'd drive each other crazy. *I'd* drive *you* crazy. I mean, you were annoyed with me because I left that picture over there." I nodded toward the living room. "I did plan on taking care of it."

"What picture?" Eric said.

"Oh," Beth said, flipping her hand in the air, "it's this silly picture of old tap shoes."

"Ballet slippers, Beth," I said. "They're ballet slippers." As a little girl, after I returned home from church, I'd pretend my Sunday dress was a tutu and hid in my room, making believe I was a ballerina. I twirled very quietly because Mother said God didn't approve of our bodies moving in anyway that wouldn't glorify Him. Still, I was hiding more from my mother's eyes than the Almighty's. Years later, when I discovered the framed poster in a head shop, I bought it and then hung it in the square of space that was my bedroom in the loft. Whenever I looked at the picture, I'd imagine it had been me who wore down those slippers.

"Slippers. Tap shoes. Whatever," Beth said, "point is, I didn't want the deaconesses having to look at it the whole time they were here for our meeting."

"Exactly," I said, "which is why we wouldn't be able to share this place."

"Because you can't have your poster in the living room?" Beth said.

"No, because I wouldn't want to have to deal with Bible studies and deaconess's meetings going on all the time. And sometimes I'd want to have

MY friends over."

"As long as they abide by the rules—"

"Rules? Beth, we're not children anymore."

Eric said, "It does seem as if selling would make more sense."

"Because of Laura, we should sell this house?" Beth walked over to the bookcase brushing her hand along the spines of Bibles, concordances and devotionals. "Mother spent her life making sure this house honored God."

I walked over to the closet, opening the door, and snatched the belt that was hanging on a hook, carrying it into the living room. Beth and Eric were silent, their expressions uneasy.

"This was part of the house, too." I held out the belt. "Or have you forgotten? And why is it still in there?"

Beth turned her head, refusing to look at it.

"Because you're too damn afraid to throw it out!"

"Don't curse," Beth said.

"Oh, it's fine what this belt was used for, but I can't say damn?" I walked over to the bookshelf. "Well, if I stay, Beth, then these have to go." Then I glimpsed the plaque at the foot of the stairs and headed toward it. "And let's take this down."

Her strident protest, "Don't touch that!" stopped me. I backed away from the wooden plaque, stenciled with the verse: *As for me and my house, we will serve the Lord. Joshua 24:15*

"Let's calm down," Eric said, coming over to me and taking the belt out of my hand. He held it for a moment, seemingly unsure where to put it, but then brought it back to the closet, tossing it in and slamming shut the door. It was the first time I noticed graying around his temples and a slight paunch.

"Why are you taking her side?" Beth said.

He took a handkerchief from his pocket and wiped his forehead. "I'm not taking anyone's side. I just don't see any other way than selling the house that'll make sense."

Beth gaped at him, her eyes filling with tears. I walked over to the couch and dropped down.

"Laura, I wish you wanted to stay," Eric said. "And, yeah, I'd like for us to be close again."

I could tell that he was sincere and it brought back memories when he and I clung to each other for support. We'd hide under either his or my bed and whisper strategies of how we were going to escape. The recollection brought my guard down. Not having planned to share my biggest news of all, I blurted, "I would love it if we were a real family. My baby would have an uncle." I hesitated, then added, "And an aunt."

Both Eric and Beth gazed at me, their mouths dropped open.

"What are you saying?" Eric said.

I paused, then said, "I'm going to have a baby." It was the first time I'd said it aloud and it sounded wonderful, a statement filled with hope, until the sound of a dish smashing to the floor came from the kitchen.

Beth sputtered, "A baby?" She put a hand over her mouth.

Eric's eyes wide, he said, "You're pregnant?"

I caught him looking at my belly. I wanted to say yes. I wanted to have felt the quickening of life growing inside me. However, I was forced to tell the truth. "Not yet," I said. "But I plan to be."

"Excuse me?" Beth said, taking a step closer.

"I don't understand," Eric said.

I gazed at the newspaper that was opened on the coffee table, at the picture of the women gathered at the rally. In spite of my own needs, I was rooting for those women. Babies should be wanted, planned; not happenstance.

"I was under the impression that you weren't dating anyone," Eric said. He turned to Beth, "You said she wasn't dating anyone."

Before Beth could reply, I said, "I'm not. And I have no intention of getting married."

"You want to have a baby *without* marriage?" Eric said.

I nodded, letting them soak in the information.

"Won't you be ashamed?" Beth said, her voice shaky, her eyes enormous in her ashen face.

"No."

"How ... do you plan...?" Eric said.

"I don't think you really want to hear all that." Actually, I didn't have a clear cut answer. Not yet. Just the night before I went to Zanzi-Bar with Gloria and Susan, and began an irresolute culling. Early in the evening things looked promising, with many of the patrons being professors and other erudite types. But as the night wore on, I discovered nothing more than a bunch of slurring drunks eager to skip the preliminaries, telling me I was "one groovy chick." The "groovy chick" went home feeling defeated.

"Well, maybe we should get this house situation straightened out first," Eric said.

Beth lunged toward him. "You're encouraging her to go ahead with this?"

"No," Eric said, "not at all." He turned to me, scowling. "But why, Laura? Why a baby?"

"Why does anyone want a baby?" I said.

Actually, when my therapist had asked me the same question, I said, "I need to understand some things."

"What kind of things?" she said.

Just things.

"This is too soon. Everything's happening too soon." Beth rushed to the picture window where a spider plant hung with hundreds of shoots suspended from it. She began to pick off the brown leaves, but then stopped and turned to face me.

"Maybe," she said, "maybe it's too soon after everything for you, too. Maybe you're just upset. Maybe losing Dad—"

"I *am* upset, but my decision has nothing to do with Dad."

"You need to think about this more clearly, Laura," Beth said.

"I've been thinking about this for years, Beth. *Years.*"

She threw up her hands. "If you want a baby so bad, why don't you adopt one?"

"You have to be rich to adopt." Jenny appeared, a dishtowel in her hand. "Or patient. They place you on a waiting list. Five years later you haven't even budged from the bottom."

I sat up straighter realizing for the first time what she was implying. I'd always just assumed that she and Eric forfeited parenthood for the ministry.

Eric walked over to Jen and put an arm around her. "Well, there is foreign adoption, but you have to be quite comfortable financially, if you want to do that."

"And if you're single," I said, "they won't even look at the application."

"See!" Beth said, "A baby needs a mother *and* a father!"

"Really?" I said. "Mom certainly didn't think so."

"What do you mean by that?" Beth said.

"I mean, I need to do this on my own."

"It's not how God had planned it!" Beth shrieked.

I raised my hand as a warning. "Let's not go there, okay?"

"Beth's face turned bright red. "Mom would be so destroyed."

"Of course she would be," I said.

Eric said, "I know Dad was waiting for a grandchild."

Jenny's face began to break up, tears coming to her eyes.

"Jenny," I said, "I'm so sorry. I don't mean--"

She pulled away from Eric, dropped the dishtowel on the floor and fled up the stairs. Eric pressed his eyes closed and sucked up some air before running after her, taking the steps by twos.

"I hope you're satisfied," Beth said.

"I didn't know," I said. "No one ever said anything about it."

"Well, if you attended prayer services, you would have known."

"Maybe I should go talk to her."

"Don't you think you've said enough?" Beth took off toward the kitchen.

I followed her, pushing through the swinging door. "It still doesn't change the fact that we need to sell the house."

"And provide you with a means to do something so sinful?" Cleaned and dried dishes were stacked on the table. Beth grabbed them and went to the cabinet.

"The money belongs to me," I said. "What I do with it is my business."

She put the dishes in the cabinet with a clatter and slammed the door. "Why must you always test my faith? Just like you did Mom's." She dashed back through the door and into the living room with me behind her. "But," she sputtered, "I will not let you frustrate ME into getting cancer."

I stopped, wondering if I'd actually heard right. I'd been accused of many things in the Sumner household before, but murder wasn't one of them. I found Beth sitting on the couch and I stood over her. "Are you saying that I gave Mom cancer? You really believe that?"

She kept her eyes down, fiddling with a loose thread on her sleeve.

"Mom thought that, didn't she?" I began pacing, shaking my head in wonder, cursing the tears that were streaming down my face. "Of course it was my fault. Of course!"

There was a spell of silence, a collection of tempers. I didn't know whether to leave or stay, but knew that leaving wouldn't bring us any closer to a resolution. I sat down on the couch next to Beth. "I guess you think Dad's heart attack was my fault, too."

"No," she said, "you could never disappoint him, no matter what you did."

But I tried, didn't I?

"His sweet little Laura," Beth said, smoothing the folds of her blue polyester dress.

Sweet? Hardly. True, it was never a question whether he favored me, but it wasn't because I was sweet and docile. No, quite the contrary. I was the entertaining rebel giving his sanctimonious wife a constant challenge while he took pleasure watching.

"Mom loved you, Laura," Beth said. "You were the one she prayed for every night—on her knees—begging for you to change your ways."

"I'm not sure what I did that was so horrible."

"And Dad," she continued, "well, he barely gave me the time of day." She wiped her eyes with the palm of her hand.

If anything, I had to agree, and it made me feel like squirming.

"You were the one he taught to swing a golf club and play chess," she said. "You and Eric."

I reached over and rested a hand on her shoulder. "Well, you were busy with other things, Beth. I mean, look at all the trophies you won memorizing all those verses. And then you went to that retreat."

I didn't think I was being hurtful, but without warning Beth's hand came up and smacked me hard across the face. It took a moment for me to realize just what had happened. I gaped at her and saw that she was just as surprised.

Dazed, I got up and went to the closet to get my purse and keys. I wanted to call up the stairs to let Eric and Jenny know I was leaving, but then thought better of it. The belt that Eric had tossed back in the closet was lying on a pair of boots. I picked it up and put it in its rightful spot on the hook before walking out the door.

Eric

The more I dabbed at Jenny's tears, the more they seemed to flow. The toilet seat cover shifted with her every movement and the faucet had a persistent leak that I couldn't stop. Sure the house needs repairs, but it's fixable. Maybe a new family and new set of values could bring it to life again and exorcise the cries and moans buried deep in the woodwork. Is the expression "born again" appropriate for a house? Another tearful shudder from Jen prompted me to crouch in front of her and dry some freshly fallen tears.

"You've got to stop punishing yourself," I said.

"How, Eric? How can I stop when everyone around me is having babies?" The toilet seat jiggled again and she adjusted herself. "I just don't understand why—"

"Maybe the Lord knows we can't afford it just now." I knew it was lame, but lately I've had to come up with excuses for His behavior. Who can blame Jenny's exasperated expression? "Jen," I said, "if Sarah was able to give Abraham a son in his old age and she was well past childbearing age, then we have nothing to worry about."

She refused to look at me. I stood up and gazed out the bathroom window. How can I really know why God does what He does? Do I have a right of appeal from His decisions? Imagine a sermon on that. The board would dismiss me in a heartbeat; pastors aren't supposed to have doubts.

The branches of the big maple tree come so close to the window that I can almost reach out and touch the buds just beginning to blossom. When I was a boy I'd manage to climb that tree, using the knots and low branches to get up high and hide in the curve of the limbs for hours. Summertime was best when I could hide in the lush leaves. Sometimes I'd stay hidden for hours in that tree.

"I'm sorry," Jen said, unraveling some toilet paper and blowing her nose.

"I don't like getting this upset. It's just I always thought we'd have children. It's something I never doubted. Isn't that what walking by faith means?"

"I never doubted it either." I hesitated, before adding, "Still don't." We'd talked about children ever since we dated, deciding that three was a nice, practical number. But, for the first few years of married life we made neither a conscious effort nor used protection, just trusted the Lord for His timing. When He wanted it to happen, it would. We just never thought He might not want it to.

During those years, I polished my preaching skills and Jen painted. She's good, too. I'm no art critic, but I like how she creates images with the ease of a brush. All from her mind. After the third year, we began to question each month's disappointment with added concern. While our prayers became more fervent, her inspiration to paint became passive, the canvasses and easel remaining untouched. And my sermons were becoming more difficult to write. It seems now our bed is no longer a shelter to embrace and give ourselves freely, but a testament of our failure.

I turned away from the window and looked at Jen. The tears had stopped, but her red, swollen face was somber. "Maybe we can call that agency again," I said.

"Which one?"

"Beginnings."

She rolled her eyes. "We can barely afford the application fee."

I shoved my hands in my pockets. "Now. But once this place is sold, I don't think that would be a problem."

That seemed to stop her, then her face clouded over again. "You heard your sister, she doesn't plan to sell."

"She's not going to have a choice. I'm sure Laura will see to that." I have to admit I was rooting for Laura not to give up as far as the house was concerned. As for having a baby the way she proposes, well I'm not sure how I feel about that. I'm not saying I don't know how I—the minister of a Bible-believing church—should feel about it, but that's another story.

Jenny stood and splashed some water on her face, and said, "Can we go home now?"

Laura

A few moments had passed since I'd backed my blue '59 Thunderbird out of the driveway. My wheel veered slightly from the path, crushing several of Beth's newly sprung crocuses. It's doubtful that Beth would believe me, but I didn't do it on purpose. At least I don't think I did; my therapist may think otherwise. Now I was on the parkway, zipping around turtle-paced Sunday drivers, as if I had somewhere important to go. A warm breeze poured through my opened windows, whipping my hair in a tangled mess, making me feel reckless. And the further I got from Seabrook, the freer I felt.

I kept my left hand on the steering wheel while stretching and turning the knob to the radio to find a station that was hard and rocking. The time it took to take my eyes from the road to see where the dial was and then back to the highway, there were red tail lights in all three lanes suddenly brightening. I slammed on the brakes, screeching within inches from the bumper in front of me. I let out a grateful sigh for the near miss, but to be stuck in traffic on a weekend was inexcusable; weekdays were simply tolerated. Then, as though my reasoning made sense to the commuter gods, the long line of cars picked up to a steady pace. It was then I spied radar tucked in a covey of trees, as if someone always needed to watch what I was doing.

Moments later, the soothing call of seagulls and ocean's whispers drew me to Jones Beach. My shoes swinging in my hand, I stepped off the boardwalk and plunged barefoot in the sand. The surface was deceptively warm, but once my feet sank deeper, the cold squished between my toes and made me flinch. Even though it was early in the season, I loped around dozens of resilient sunbathers sprawled on their blankets, before I reached the water's edge.

The misty air salted my skin. I sat down on the damp sand, and watched as the torpid waves strolled up then coiled back out to sea. They have the magic to lull me, to help me sort out what had just transpired.

During Dad's wake and funeral it made sense to stay on Long Island rather than travel back and forth to the city. But now that it's over, every exhausting detail, I wanted to move forward with my plan. With both Mom and Dad gone, her with her severe expectations and he with his detached nonchalance, it leaves only what I consider opportunity. A new beginning. A baby. I hugged myself with the thought.

Babies grow up to be people, my therapist had said during our last session.

I know.

There's still a chance you'll meet someone and fall in love.

I don't think so.

Know what i think? I think you are trying to understand what a mother's love is supposed to feel like and the only way to do so is for you to become a mother.

Okay.

Laura.

I said okay.

As if waves were memories, Beth's accusations beckoned me back to the aching months when Mother was dying. Skin sagging from her brittle bones and cheeks and eyes sunk in a gray face, she'd looked to be already on the other side.

"If only I could see a change in you before…" She'd leave the thought suspended between us while I wordlessly swabbed her watery blue eyes.

"Proverbs promises if I train up a child in the way they should go, they will not depart from it. Let me see that promise, Laura, before…"

That's when I'd say I had to go before traffic builds up, glancing at my watch to feign a look of shock.

"Don't let the devil have his way, Laura."

"I have to finish this article I'm working on," I'd reply.

"Why must you cause me so much aggravation?"

"I'm sorry."

"The wages of sin is death, Laura—"

I have to go find a fucking wall to pound.

Eventually, I would escape, but guilt would always bring me back. One Saturday afternoon, when the guilt was again victorious, I walked in while some deacons were laying hands on my mother's supine body. Beth was kneeling at the foot of the bed, her swaying arms thrust toward the heavens while a hum of pleading filled the room. I turned and went downstairs to the kitchen. Dad was sitting at the table, staring into his cup of filmy coffee. I poured myself a cup and sat down with him. I reached out and rested my hand on his. Neither of us spoke.

Once I heard the deacons thump down the stairs and out the door, I went back up to the bedroom.

"A miracle has happened," my mother said, extending a long, bony arm toward me.

I saw no miraculous afterglow and felt no energy in the room, but forced a smile, taking the few steps to her bedside. Beth was sitting on the edge, tears streaming down her cheeks, while she caressed Mother's wan face.

All I could manage to say was, "That's good, Mom. Really good."

She closed her eyes and, barely above a whisper, said, "Soon, I'll be able to get on my knees again to pray for your soul."

I turned and walked out.

A few weeks later when Dad came home from work, he found Mom in bed, an opened Bible next to her lifeless body.

A foamy wave crawled up, tickled my toes, then scurried back out to sea. I let it take the memory. Drown it.

I tried to summon better thoughts, remembering how I felt when I'd announced that I was going to have a baby. It was such an optimistic statement, but to think that I was hoping to succeed where Eric and Jenny failed. At thirty years old, my biological clock was clanging. Not to mention that I didn't yet have a volunteer to help me. *Volunteer* was how I referenced the man who would agree to all my stipulations, as if he existed.

The ocean air began to chill me and I looked around to see that many of the sunbathers had vanished. I stood and brushed the sand from my backside and headed toward the parking lot.

Beth

Eric backed his rickety Impala out of the driveway and I gave a final wave goodbye to him and Jenny, even though I'll be seeing them in a little while at evening service. There were Sundays when I could convince them to stay the whole afternoon, right up until it was time to leave for church. But today, as soon as they came back downstairs, Jenny's eyes red-rimmed, Eric said he thought it best if they went back to the parsonage to rest for awhile.

It was exactly what I thought he'd say.

So, before they'd come downstairs and right after Laura stormed out, I set the table for dessert. I even used Mom's good china. Sure enough, once Eric saw the cake and coffee spread out, he mumbled to Jenny that maybe they should stay since I went to so much trouble. I have to admit that Jenny didn't look too thrilled and didn't even take any dessert.

Once the car was out of sight, I ambled back into the house and began to clean off the dining room table. All through dessert Eric kept hinting how the house was too big for just one person. I, on the other hand, tried to bring the conversation back to Laura and how insensitive she was, not to mention that what she wanted to do was beyond reason. I didn't think it necessary to mention how she'd managed to rile me enough to raise my hand to her.

After I put the dirty dishes in the sink, I went back into the living room and pulled out my favorite Bible, the KING JAMES VERSION, from the bookshelf and began leafing through it. The pages were so dog-eared they kept falling out. I lugged it to the couch and sat down, opening God's word to where the Old Testament ends and the New begins. Tucked between the pages was one of my favorite photos. I took it out and gazed at it.

There she is, the woman who wanted nothing more than to get her three children through the gates of heaven. Where we're going will last a lot longer than where we are now. I closed my eyes and repeated one of mother's favorite verses from Corinthians: "While we look not at the things which are seen, but at the things which are not seen: for the things which are seen are temporal: but the things which are not seen are eternal."

I looked around the room. Sure, it could use a fresh coat of paint and new carpet, but I figured it would always be home to me until the Lord decides to take me.

Whenever I feel discouraged or afraid, I take out this picture and remind myself of all the things Mother taught me. How righteous she appears, her head held high, an arm around my waist. I was holding up a blue ribbon for the camera and looked to be about fifteen. I deserved that ribbon, too, the hours I stayed in my room memorizing all those verses until they rolled off my tongue easy as pie.

Neither of us is smiling and I wonder why we weren't encouraged to do so.

Hold that ribbon high, Beth.

Just then, there is a popping sound and flash of the camera. I felt a sickness come over me. Not a stomachache, but something deeper than that. An uneasiness. I tucked the photograph back into the Bible and dropped to my knees. Using the couch for support, I tried to pray.

I asked the Lord to take away the gnawing feeling, but instead breathing became difficult.

Pray, Beth, pray, I tell myself.

I try, groping for phrases, words, anything that would form a prayer, but nothing connects. Images, hideous images, muddled my thoughts. And there is that pop and flash again. I beg for it to stop.

Pray.

And once again, I tried. But the words come out garbled, hollow. I dropped my head on the cushion and sobbed.

CHAPTER TWO

Laura

Monday morning with a deadline to meet and I was unable to tap out anything that made sense. On the train ride in to Manhattan, I jotted down notes comparing the mind-boggling present-day space program to Columbus discovering the Americas, but Mike, my boss, thought that since I was the only woman on staff, I should work on a more feminine topic. "Let one of the guys cover that," he said. I picked up my bagel and ripped into it, cursing Mike with every bite and swallow.

Loans. Apartments. Babies. Those were the topics that kept rattling around in my head until someone knocked on my door.

"How about I write about sanitary napkins?" I shouted. "That feminine enough for you?"

The door edged open. "Uh, this a bad time?"

I looked up to see Dawn's brown face poke in.

"Oh gosh," I said, dropping my head into my hands. "I thought you were Mike. Please, come in."

She walked in with her baby in tow.

"Aisia!" I squealed. I jumped up, prompting Dawn to hand her over. After a moment's delaying, she did and, immediately, Aisia's bottom lip began to quiver.

"Oh, no, no, no," I said, bouncing the baby with a button for a nose and a wisp of hair gathered in the tiniest of pink bows. She reached for her mother, but I was determined to appease her.

"Hoo … wee ooo … ba … by, ba … by." I danced around my desk. "Hoo … wee ooo … ba … by, ba … by."

Big brown eyes studied me with the most dubious of expressions, but she'd stopped whimpering. I continued in my song.

"I swear, girl, you are crazy," Dawn said. "Didn't your mama ever teach you real lullabies?"

I rubbed the baby's cheek against mine. I never talked about my past with those who were a part of my present. Except my therapist. I kept singing while Aisia gurgled, drooled and pulled strands of my hair. Finally, I said, "We miss you around here."

"Believe it or not, there are some days I miss being a secretary myself," Dawn said. "Even with Mike and his nasty attitude."

Writing a column could be done pretty much anywhere, even from home, which is what I was counting on once I had my baby. Better yet, a lucrative book deal could support me and I could drop my position at *Day's Notice*, which reminded me that it was time to get in touch with Loren.

"Well," Dawn said, reaching over for her little girl, "she has a doctor's appointment, but I wanted to stop in and say hi."

"Can you imagine life without her now?" I said, not ready to hand over the baby.

"Not without palpitations." She scooped up Aisia and straightened the sleeve of her polo top, as if I'd messed up what had been perfection. "She was an unexpected surprise, but we worked it out."

After a kiss on the cheek goodbye, I watched as they went to the bank of elevators before shutting my door. I went back to my desk. The blank piece of paper in my typewriter taunted me. *Something feminine.*

What would I name *my* baby? I reached for my pen and began scratching some names in my opened notebook. How come there were no more Gertrudes or Ethels? Zekes or Chesters?

I sat up straight and poised myself over the typewriter and clacked out: A ROSE BY ANY OTHER NAME. Not bad. And five hundred words later I had the first draft to my column, along with the need for a break.

Not much later, I was walking through the revolving doors of the Manhattan Savings Bank, an intimidating marble cavern from shiny floor to spiraling pillars. I approached the first desk in the chain of command. A balding man looked up, giving me the once over. Briefly, while requesting a loan application, I wondered about his virility.

"Loan?" he said. "What type?"

"Apartment."

"For renting?" he said with a scowl.

"No, I mean to buy. I do have an account here," I said, hoping the paltry amount I had in savings wouldn't work against me.

"Oh, then you'll need to speak to Mr. Lyon." He stretched his neck. "He's right over there and it looks like he's just about finished with his client."

"I'm really just on a lunch break, so if there are some forms---"

"Oh, he's free now," he said, as a couple stood and shook Mr. Lyon's hand. "I'll bring you over."

I followed the man who introduced me to Mr. Lyon, and then shot me a wink before going back to his desk. Fifteen minutes later I was still trying to get the loan officer to understand exactly what I needed. His unsmiling face took on a look of impatience. Straightening his tie, he said, "As I've been trying to explain, Miss Sumner, you do not have a firm idea yet how much money you need because you simply do not understand the Real Estate market." He tapped his pen on his desk. "And we certainly cannot sit here and say, yes, you'll be approved until we have some idea of what we're working with."

I shifted in my chair, scooting closer to the edge of his desk. "See," I said, "once I sell my book and my parents' house gets sold then I'll know how much I can put down and then—"

"We can't go on the what-ifs."

"But I'd just like an idea of what's available to me."

"Perhaps then we should look for something that doesn't rely on the … what-ifs."

"We?"

He rolled his eyes. "Look, Miss Sumner, I have a ton of work I must get to."

I purposely gave the single sheet of paper on his desk a long stare.

"Now, my suggestion is to look in the real estate section of the paper and see what you think you might be able to manage, being a single woman and all."

"Is that going to be a problem?" I said. "My being single?"

"Well." He coughed, then said, "Why don't you come back after you do what I suggested. Then we can see what we could work out." He stood and stuck out his hand. I barely grazed it before walking away, the bald-headed fellow now in deep discussion with some woman whose mini-dress exposed legs that didn't seem to end.

The lunch crowd was a jumble of sounds at Sam's Pub, dishes clattering over the hum of conversation punctuated by boisterous laughter. I had a newspaper opened across the wobbly table and was scanning the lengthy listings, not sure what was more daunting—the multitude of choices, all hyped to sound spacious and in a great location—or the blatant asking prices.

The waitress breezed by, dropping my order on top of the paper, causing the table to rock and some Mountain Dew to spill. It had to be the warmth of such people that explained such choice real estate. One bite of my sandwich and chicken salad regurgitated from the bread and leaked onto my hands and newspaper. A recognizable laugh caused me to look up to see Stefanos standing over me, appearing taller than his six-foot frame. My face warmed and I began to wipe up the mess.

"So, may I join you?" He pointed to the empty chair across from me.

I folded the paper and nodded for him to sit. I tried not to survey his brown eyes and black curly hair pulled into a ponytail.

"I went looking for you at your office," he said, a hint of a Greek accent in his voice. "They said you went to lunch. I took a shot and came here."

"Some shot," I said. The pub is across the street from my office. "I know I owe back rent. I'll try to get it to you soon." I took another bite of my sandwich.

He shook his head. "This isn't about the money. Besides, I've just been commissioned to do the lobbies on the floors of the new high rise going up in lower Manhattan. They want my interpretation of the century's greatest events."

"What about inspiration? Isn't that what you told me always fueled you?"

"After I saw what they wanted to pay, inspiration abounded!" He broke into a hearty laugh.

The bleach-blond waitress's previous whirlwind suddenly came to a steady, gazing calm. "Excuse me," she said, resting her thigh against the table, spilling my soda once again. "Could I get you something?"

I saw how his eyes looked her over when he ordered water with lemon.

"Water with lemon?" I said. "Since when?"

He patted his flat stomach. A trace of ripples could be seen beneath his black T-shirt.

"Anything to eat?" the waitress said.

"Dry tuna on lettuce sounds good," he said.

She jotted his order down, gave him a flirty smile, then sashayed away.

"Water? Dry tuna?"

He shrugged.

"No more ale and burgers with a side of greasy fries, huh?"

His smile was a smoldering glow.

"*Something's* inspiring you."

He lifted the edge of the paper. "Real Estate?" He dropped back in to the curve of his chair. "What's going on, Laura?"

I refused to meet his gaze. "I need a place to live."

"I didn't kick you out."

I felt the anger rising within me, the chicken salad churning.

He leaned in, his dark eyes pressing down on me. "You didn't call, didn't let me know what the hell you were doing."

I met his gaze. "I figured you had your hands full." I had to look away, settle my sights on a neon Schaefer sign. One of the E's was flickering.

"Aunt Angie asks about you. She got your thank you card for the flowers."

My throat started to close up.

"I told you I'd be there for you, if you wanted," he said.

"I didn't realize I had to ask." I was reminded of my therapist's unconvincing words: *Not all men are selfish, Laura.*

The waitress reappeared, brushing her midriff against Stefano's hairy arm as she placed his water down. She lingered for a moment, until he reached across the table, taking my hand.

"I did have a reason to come looking for you, but it wasn't about the rent." His thumb caressed my pinkie.

Maybe he did care; maybe his latest conquest was over. Maybe he wanted the same thing I wanted.

He said, "I'm getting married."

I pulled my hand free. "Married?" I said, the wind knocked out of me. "Wow."

"She's a singer. Sings at a jazz club in the Village."

"Wow."

"Yeah," he said, beaming.

"Think she can keep you honest?"

"What's that supposed to mean?"

"I think you know what it means."

"Laura, what you and I had was nothing more than two people who took advantage of a good situation. I love Coral."

"Coral?"

"That's her name," he said. "Coral Breeze."

"Coral Breeze?"

He gushed. "Beautiful, isn't it?"

"If she's a tropical drink."

"Funny," he said. "You have to hear her sing. She can scat better than Ella."

"You should let Ella's people know."

The waitress appeared with his tuna platter. She barely looked my way when she asked if I needed anything else. I shook my head and was rewarded with the check.

"Mmm," Stefanos said, pulling out his wallet. He slid the top picture out of the plastic sleeve, started to hand it to me, then withdrew it. "Your hands."

"What?"

"They're probably sticky."

It would have been effortless to smack him with my sticky hands, but I restrained myself, which would make my therapist proud. Taking my napkin, I rubbed each finger with exaggerated care.

He handed me the photo as if it were sacred, and said, "Her brother snaps a pretty good picture."

It helps when the image is flawless, when long, thick sable-hair cascades around a structured bronze face. Coral appeared at ease, her curvy copper-colored body poured into a tight-fitting dress, pressed against a grinning Stefanos.

"Why are you showing me this?" I said, handing the picture back.

"Because I'm in love! I thought you'd be happy for me. God, Laura, you act like we were exclusive. You didn't come back, remember?"

You were supposed to run after me.

"I mean, it's not like I don't care about you. I want you to be as happy as I am."

Happy? Let's see, my life is filled with searching for a place i'm not sure i can afford, with a loan i have no idea i can get, so i can raise a baby i haven't yet conceived by a man whom i doubt exists. Oh, stefanos, things were never better for me. Really!

I said, "I guess you cornered the market on happiness."

"Well," he said, "don't want to keep you any longer. Just wanted to tell you what was going on." He stabbed his pile of tuna and took a healthy bite.

I was yesterday's news being given my notice and, obediently, I got up to leave. When I tossed my money on the table, he grabbed my hand, bringing it to his lips. "I'll never forget us," he said.

I pulled my hand away, knowing once his eyes settled back on his tropical drink I'd be a faded memory. Oh, hell, I already was. I nudged through the crowd, slipping on my sunglasses. A blast of bright, warm sunshine met me once I pushed through the door. Instead of crossing the street to my office, I hailed a cab.

A short time later, one pulled up and I climbed in, giving the address to my therapist. Maybe she would explain why I felt the way I did.

CHAPTER THREE

Beth

Without a doubt God is disappointed with the way I feel, but I cannot help be grateful that the school week is finally over. I am expected to look at each day as an opportunity to share the love of God to my students, but lately they are nothing more than distracted and restless. My voice is hoarse from having to scream at them to behave, while many went home with disciplinary notes to be signed by their parents. Years ago, I thought teaching at Jordan River Christian School would be the perfect, tranquil job. Just goes to show how the devil likes to test the faithful over and over again, trying to break us down. That's what I'd told Mr. Hanson, the principal, when he'd asked to see me just this morning. He thinks I may be a bit uptight.

"Uptight?" I said. It seems everyone was using that word lately. That's when I blamed God's adversary for trying to trip me up, making the students test my patience. But Mr. Hanson had the audacity to laugh and say that he thought it was more from the students' eagerness to get outside in the sunshine after being cooped up all winter.

"Just relax this weekend," he said to me. "And aren't you heading up VBS this year at the church?"

I nodded.

"And you still teach Sunday school?"

Another nod.

"Maybe you should think about letting someone else pitch in. Give yourself a break."

I said, "The Sovereign Lord is my strength; he makes my feet like the feet of a deer and enables me to go on the heights."

He didn't say another word, but patted me on the shoulder and then walked down the hall back to his office.

Now it was Friday evening and I was home in my bedroom preparing my lesson plan for Sunday school. I sighed and rubbed my eyes. The bright light of the lamp beamed on my open Bible as I copied II Thessalonians 1:8, 9 on an index card:

IN FLAMING FIRE TAKING VENGEANCE ON THEM THAT KNOW NOT GOD, AND THAT OBEY NOT THE GOSPEL OF OUR LORD JESUS CHRIST: WHO SHALL BE PUNISHED WITH EVER-LASTING DESTRUCTION FROM THE PRESENCE OF THE LORD, AND FROM THE GLORY OF HIS POWER.

I underlined the word "obey" three times—in red—hoping the children would heed the warning.

I just couldn't understand why Laura didn't.

And there it happened again. Like most of the week, my thoughts keep going back to my sister—my belligerent, ungodly sister. I haven't seen her all week. We somehow managed to miss each other. Okay, so maybe I've been going to bed especially early to avoid another confrontation. But who can blame me? Praying has become difficult lately, but I still know what He wants and I'm told that giving the loan to Laura will only help her continue in sin. I must not provide the means or, I too, will be culpable.

Each night I hear Laura clamor around downstairs in the kitchen, heating up leftovers. Sometimes I forget Dad is gone and cook the same amount I always did, which works out fine since Laura's here now. I just don't understand why she doesn't want to stay. There's always a meal waiting for her and a warm bed. Who in their right mind would leave the safety of home and go out trying to find trouble? Mom always said that out there, out beyond our front door, was the pathway to destruction and it sure looks like Laura found it.

I can scarce think about how she plans to do what she wants to do. I cinch my bathrobe collar. Still, women do it. And, find it enjoyable! Even women in the congregation. Sometimes during our deaconess meetings one of them brings up how by day's end she's too exhausted to do anything with her husband; heavens—as if exhaustion were the only reason to avoid all that. Makes me grateful I'm not married. Still, I have questions.

Church folks have their pastor they can go to for help, but very few church folks have a brother standing at the lectern every Sunday. That's fine, I suppose, because I take my concerns and lay them at the Lord's feet. And he carries them for me, just like he did that cross. If Laura understood that, she wouldn't need to spend gads of money talking to some psychiatrist. Lord knows what she goes on about. Mom used to say that Laura had the face of an angel, with her creamy complexion and clear blue eyes, but the devil lived inside. I wasn't blessed with great looks, but great looks aren't what gets us through the gates of heaven.

Hold that ribbon high, Beth.

I catch my breath. I rustle the pages. I missed the sound of Dad's TV coming from his bedroom. I got up and crossed the hallway. His room smelled of Old Spice. I turned the television on and found a basketball game in progress. I turned up the volume and went back to my room, landing on my chair, attempting to focus on the lesson plan.

Imagine, giving up teaching, as Mr. Hanson suggested. When September rolls around each year and the students get their class assignments and find me standing in the classroom, I hear how they groan. It doesn't bother me, though. My reply is always the same: "You can run, but you cannot hide." The confusion on their faces makes me feel prophetic. We all need guidance to get where we should be and I thank God I can be of service in that department.

I sat up straight, hearing Laura's car pull in the driveway. She's early tonight. I clicked off my lamp and scrambled into bed. In one swift move, I crawled under the covers, leaving my bathrobe on. The sound of my breathing fills the room so I try to hold my breath.

The front door opened and closed. Instead of heading to the kitchen, Laura is coming up the stairs. I then realized that I've left the TV on in Dad's room. It's too risky to try to run across the hall to turn it off. Her footsteps stop. I peeked from under my covers and see Laura's shadowy figure in the doorway.

"You listening to the game?"

I pretend I'm asleep until she says she knows I'm awake.

I mumbled that I forgot to turn it off.

"It's okay," she said. "I miss him, too." Her shadow disappeared and I hear the creak of Dad's bed and the sudden roar of the crowd. I roll on my side, squeezing my eyes shut and, in desperate whispers, call out to my Lord.

Laura

I leaned against my bedroom window and looked out at the Saturday morning downpour; an appropriate ending to a less-than-perfect week. It began on Monday with Mr. Lyon's chilly response to my trying to get a home loan followed by Stefanos' "good news" and went downhill from there. It didn't help to have my therapist ask me, "Why do you think you feel that way, Laura? Or "How would you have liked Stefanos to tell you?" I reminded my therapist that I was seeking answers not questions and cut the impromptu session short.

Then, all week long in between forming sentences that will hopefully become a fascinating column justifying my presence at *Day's Notice*, I did some apartment shopping. I dashed from one end of town to the other, hoping the apartment that was *"Priced To Sell"* or *"In Mint Condition"* would be *"The One."* My most recent venture was the most discouraging.

I'd followed the Realtor into a shoddy building, the rickety elevator shimmying us to the ninth floor. When the agent unlocked the door and flicked on the light, our unexpected visit caused mayhem for hundreds of skittering cockroaches. I did an immediate about face, hearing the crunch under my heel as I ran back outside.

Friday I decided to take a break from apartment shopping and came back to Long Island early with several different papers to scour the personal columns. After watching some basketball, I curled up in bed to peruse the listings of the lovelorn, hoping to find someone whose message would hint at what I wanted.

It wasn't long before I sent the papers sailing across the room.

According to their syrupy message, every man was ready to commit himself to the right woman. What did I expect them to say, though: Have sperm, will travel?

The rain had a mesmerizing effect on me and I didn't budge when I heard the telephone ring. A moment later, Beth called from downstairs saying that it was for me. I went into the hall, scuffing over to the washed-out pine stand. On its bottom shelf was the white pages from 1958, now yellow with age. I picked up the receiver to the clunky black phone.

"Well, finally. I was ready to hire a private detective to track you down."

"Loren, hi! How are you?"

"How am I? Annoyed, is how I am."

"Why?" I leaned my back against the wall and slid down to the floor, expecting to hear that he wasn't able to sell *The Pink Goose*.

"The question is, why haven't you returned my calls?"

"What calls?"

He sighed. "Between the idiots who work at that asshole paper of yours and your sister, you'd think someone would've told you I called!"

"You talked to Beth?" I said.

"I talked to everyone, trying to find you," Loren said. "Why don't you hire a goddamn answering service? Oh, fuck it. No one ever calls back, anyway. Here I try to rush to get you an answer and then…."

Loren was famous for his tirades. I pictured his lanky body pacing as far as the phone cord would permit, then back again, while he smoothed his pewter-colored hair. He'd mellow soon. He always does.

"So, how have you been, darling?" He'd mellowed. "I do have some good news for you."

"Really?"

He raised his voice again. "Really? Where the hell you been? Did you move back there for good?"

"I'm trying to get back into the city," I said. "So, tell me, did you sell it?"

"Not only did I sell it, they want to release it in the fall."

"They want to publish the Goose in the *fall?* That's fast." I smiled.

"I told you it was no question about selling, but they snatched it up. Oh ye of little faith!" He chuckled. "You established yourself, now things are beginning to take off."

Part one accomplished.

"Yeah, but I thought *Ghosts Can Be Real* and *Trying To Be Big* would take off."

"Well, *The Pink Goose* will. I'd like to meet face to face. Talk about it. What're you doing tonight?"

"It's a Saturday night, Loren. What do you think I'm doing?"

"Oh, you got a date."

"No."

He chortled. "So, let's get together and catch up."

"Where and when?"

"Well, Esther has another damn charity event and if I can use you as an excuse, I won't need to go with her. I have to bring her to the Waldorf so how's about we meet at the Bull and Bear? Eightish?"

"Sounds good."

"Laura, I feel real good about the proposed plans, major book tour, they're talking."

"Really?"

"Hell," he said, "pretty soon you'll do so damn good you can dump that piddly-assed job at that rinky dink paper."

"It would be nice to actually make some money," I said, thinking mortgage application.

"See you tonight and don't stand me up!" He hung up without saying goodbye.

I put the phone into the cradle. Perhaps I'd get a nice advance, enough for a down payment. Before I had time to think much about it, the phone rang again. I picked it up and said hello.

"Laura? Stefanos."

"What?" I said, my tone cold.

"Come on, babe, don't be that way."

I sucked up some air. "Would Coral appreciate you calling me babe?"

"Listen, I know I told you the other day not to worry about the back rent, but I could really use it. The wedding is costing more than we expected." After a moment's silence, he said, "Laura?"

"The check'll be in the mail."

"Oh, come on. You sound pissed."

"Because I am."

"I want to still be friends, Laura."

"Friends?"

"Listen please keep August 28th opened."

"Why?"

"I want you to come to the wedding."

"Are you kidding?"

"No, I'm not. Besides, Aunt Angie would love it if you were there."

"That's not fair to say."

"But it's true."

"I'll have to check my calendar," I said.

"Well, I'd really like you to be there."

To rub my nose in it? I told him I had to get off the phone and then slammed down the receiver. I pulled myself up from the floor and traipsed back to my bedroom, making my bed by pounding my pillows with my fist then ramming the floral comforter into a slapdash tuck. I wandered back to the window, watching the rain turn to hail. I hoped for the same weather on August 28th then idled my way downstairs. Beth was in the living room, watering the spider plant hanging near the picture window.

"I can't believe how many shoots it has," I said. Every muscle in Beth's plump body stood at attention, but she didn't turn, just kept trickling water into the ceramic pot.

"And Mom gave so many away, too," she said. "I guess it's her legacy."

Among other things. I strolled into the living room. "I wouldn't mind one of those shoots myself."

Beth glanced over her shoulder. "I don't think it'd survive with the amount of light that gets into your room."

"I mean when I move."

She sighed. "I just wish you didn't feel you had to." She set the water can down and began tweaking off dead leaves.

"Well, I have to. Meantime, will you please remember to give me my messages? It could be something important."

"Sorry, but I have a lot of things going on, too."

"Okay, but it's just something else that proves our sharing a house won't work."

She tossed the dead leaves in a wastebasket.

"Beth?"

"Do we have to discuss it now? I'm just not ready to think about all that. She turned, sucking up some air, then said, "I did want to say that I was sorry about the other day ... I ... I didn't mean to slap you. I...."

"You slapped me?" I said. "I didn't know you slapped me. I thought it was a mosquito."

She rolled her eyes at the childish taunting reference, then looked me up and down. "You may want to get dressed."

"Why?" Often, back at the loft, I'd remain in my sweats the entire weekend.

"Well, Jenny's coming over."

"I doubt she'll care, Beth. Any coffee left?" I said.

She hesitated, then said, "I just polished off the last cup. More'll have to be made."

"No problem." I headed to the kitchen where I found the table heaped with palm fronds and a pile of ribbons. I picked one up and read the block letters printed on a shiny blue strip: *Hosanna: Blessed is the King of Israel that cometh in the name of the Lord. John 12:13.*

Beth pushed through the swinging door. "Oh, Jenny's coming over soon to help me with those—they have to be ready for tomorrow."

I went to the counter and scooped some ground coffee into a filter.

"Tomorrow's Palm Sunday, you know," Beth said.

"Right."

"Remember when Mom had us make all those crosses from palm leaves?" Beth said. "And then we got to hand them out to everyone?"

I turned the tap on full force. The memory for me wasn't warm and pastel-colored.

Not more than about four years old, I said to my mother, "I don't wanna do that. I wanna paint eggs."

"That's not what the holy day is about."

"This is stupid," I said, brushing the pile of palm leaves from the kitchen table and onto the floor. The memory of what occurred next is vivid, painful—a little girl's longing for a colorful world confined to sepia tones.

I put the coffee pot on the burner and lit it, just as the doorbell rang.

"Must be Jenny," Beth chirped, darting out of the kitchen. Moments later, she returned. Jenny was right behind and soaking wet. She took the dish towel I handed her and squeezed water from her hair.

"Nasty out there, huh?" I said.

"Flooding in some parts," she said.

I nodded. "Listen," I said, putting some bread into the toaster, "I didn't mean to upset you the other day."

Jenny's face reddened. "You didn't upset me."

"Of course she did," Beth said.

Jenny shot Beth a look of annoyance. "I was just feeling emotional, I guess."

"Well, I'm sorry that, you know, it's not happening—"

"Let's forget all about that just now," Beth said. "Jenny and I have a lot to get done here." She sat her lump of a body down at the table and picked up a ribbon. Jenny joined her and the two began crafting crosses out of palm leaves and ribbons. With a glass of orange juice, buttered toast and coffee, I sat down with them, clearing a small space for myself.

Beth sniffed. "This brings back such memories. We were so cute, all dressed up in our Sunday best."

"Mom sure liked to make us look like the perfect family, didn't she?" I said.

Beth gazed at me. "What's that mean?"

"It's funny," Jenny interjected in haste, "being a missionary kid you would've thought we did things like this, but we really didn't."

"No?" Beth said. "What did you do?"

I ate in silence while Jenny and Beth talked. Once I was finished I took a paper napkin from the plastic holder and wiped my hands. I then picked up a palm leaf and ribbon.

"What are you doing?" Beth said.

"Helping."

Beth dropped her hands to her lap and her bottom lip began to quiver. "Oh, Laura."

"I was going to wash my car, but don't see that happening in this weather," I said. "Besides, we could talk about the house situation." I hadn't planned to say that, it just sort of slipped out, but then I saw Jenny's anxious expression and realized she wouldn't want to be in the middle of any such discussion. "I guess it would be better, though, if Eric was here."

"Yes!" Jenny said. "That's a good idea. Why don't we talk about Easter dinner?"

"Easter?" I said. I hadn't spent Easter or any holiday with the family in years.

"We're having it at the parsonage, Laura," Jenny said. "I hope you can come."

"Are you sure you wouldn't want me to cook?" Beth said. "There's so much more room here."

"No, I'd love to host it," Jenny said. "It'll be just us." She hesitated, before adding, "And maybe Deacon Don."

Beth's hand began to shake as she attempted to tie the ribbon in a bow.

"Are you okay?" I said.

"Fine!" Beth said.

"Unless you'd rather we didn't invite him, Beth," Jenny said.

Without looking up, Beth said, "Why would I care either way? Goodness, Jenny, it's your home. You can invite whoever you want."

"So," Jenny said to me, "think you can make it?"

I wanted to say no. I wanted to have a good enough reason to say no. Instead, I said, "Sure. I'll bring the dessert."

I spotted Loren nursing a drink at the bar at the Bull and Bear. He looked to be so deep in thought it was downright evil of me to sneak up behind him like a whirlwind and throw myself over him.

"Christ!" he said. "Give someone a clue, will ya?"

I kissed his flushed cheek and he motioned for me to sit on the stool next to his.

"You drive in?" he said.

"If you can call it that. Doesn't drive imply moving forward? Took me over twenty minutes alone to get through the tunnel."

"We got reservations for nine, but let's get you a drink." He nodded to the bartender. "Can't believe you're still out there in sunny Seabrook."

"No more than I can." I popped a cashew from a bowl of nuts into my mouth. "I plan to be back here soon. I hate the commute." Which was why I brought my overnight bag filled with the necessities. Before coming to the bar I checked into a room. As pricey as it was, I needed a break from Beth. The bartender strolled over and I ordered a red wine.

"So, you're not planning on going back to the loft, back to that sono-fa—"

"No. I want to buy my own place, so I cannot wait to hear about the offer we got." Earlier, I'd mulled over whether or not to tell Loren my seminal scheme and the scales of logic tipped to keep my lip zipped side. Even though it was the '60s, and all about free love, Loren was still old school. My wine was placed before me and I took a sip.

"So, like I told you, they want the book to come out in the fall. And I told them you were working madly on the next one." He gave me an anticipative look. "They bought it as a series."

"That's great!" I said. "I'm working on it. Well, I had been before…."

He put his hand on mine. "I know, it's been a rough time. I told 'em that, too."

I nodded.

"They're also proposing some other stuff. Nothing's firm yet, but ideas to ponder." He looked into his glass, swirling the ice.

"And?"

"Well, I don't want to get your hopes too high, but there's some pretty big talk going on about this book."

"It's a kid's book, Loren."

"Don't sell yourself short. They're saying it's fresh, the best thing to come along since … since…."

"Cat in the Hat?"

He rolled his eyes. "Well, maybe not that big, but here's the pitch: They are considering making an animation starring your Pink Goose."

"Just like the Grinch!"

"Will you stop that, already?" he said.

"So my goose gets a Saturday morning cartoon sponsored by all those sugar-coated cereals. What should we call it, 'Goose Gets Down'?"

Loren shook his head. "Go ahead, joke around. But I did right by you this time."

"You did," I said, raising my glass to him.

"First, we're going to get the book out there, get some focus on it, build up some steam. Then—"

"Loren?" a voice a short distance away said. "That you old chap?" Loren turned. "So it bloody well is!" A man approached the bar.

"Peter!" Loren jumped up and pumped the man's hand. "I didn't know you were in town."

"Indeed," he said, raking his hand through thick blond hair. "Trying to get back into the swing of things."

Loren patted Peter on the back. "It'll come, give it time." Peter eyed me with a look of suspicion and Loren said, "Oh! This is Laura. She's a writer, too." He turned to me and said, "Cynthia's Peter's agent."

"Cynthia?"

"In my agency, the loudmouth across the hall."

I nodded and extended my hand.

"Peter Collins," Peter said. "Certainly hope I'm not interrupting anything."

"Well, I was just filling Laura in on the deal I got for her. Esther's up in the Grand Ballroom for some charity gig. Why don't you join us?" Loren said.

Peter glanced at his watch. "I'm s'posed to meet up with dinner companions here, but I am a trifle early." Peter took the stool next to Loren.

"So, Laura," Peter said, leaning over to see past Loren, "you from around here?"

I nodded. "You're a long way from home."

"Oh, just across the pond," he said. "And you're a writer, as well?"

"Some days I'm not so sure," I said.

"I'm seeing a jolly good lot of those days myself lately, which explains why I haven't gone to see Cynthia yet, let her know I'm in town."

"She'll be eager to see you," Loren said.

"Afraid there's nothing to show her just yet."

While the bartender took Peter's drink order I tried to get a better look at him, to see if there was a signifying ring on his left hand, with little success. "So," I said, "would I recognize your work?"

Peter picked up his scotch on the rocks and swilled it down. He then said, "I write under a nom de plume." He looked across the bar and waved to a well-preserved patrician-looking couple just entering. "Well, that certainly didn't provide us much time to chat," he said, standing and giving Loren a hasty hand shake. "Be sure to give Esther my best." He took my hand and said something about it being nice meeting me before dashing over to the couple.

I turned to Loren and said, "So, who is he?"

"Some Brit who's making Cynthia crazy."

"I mean, what name does he write under?"

Just then the hostess appeared and said our table was ready.

While Loren and I trailed behind the young woman, I began to wonder about Peter. He did look a bit older than the ideal man I had in mind. I guess he'd be about forty. I didn't get a second look, though, because we'd reached our table without crossing his path.

After we ordered our dinner, I waited for Loren to get back to our conversation about the publisher's plans, but was surprised to hear him mentioning Peter.

"Good to see him around again," he said, almost in a whisper. "He'd been keeping himself locked away in London after his wife died."

So there'd been a wife. "How'd she die?"

"Head-on collision. Knocked him for a loop. Thing is, he was supposed to be with her but had a deadline, so he stayed home to write."

"Guess something like that would create a block."

"Cynthia's afraid there'll be no more Nancy Greenly novels."

"Nancy Greenly. *He's* Nancy Greenly?"

Loren nodded. "See," he said, "a few years back, Peter wrote a romance and it was purchased with high expectations. But it bombed. Well, more like fizzled. Some survey showed that women love those kind of books—romance, smoldering sex—but they are more comfortable reading them when the author is a woman."

"Or at least having them believe it's a woman."

"Yup. So, he pens another romance, but this time it goes on the shelf as Nancy Greenly. Takes off like a rocket."

"And there's such a mystery about her, which helps him."

"Yeah, but now there may not be anymore Nancy Greenly novels, if he doesn't break through his block."

"How long since his wife died?" I said, just as the waiter appeared with our appetizers.

"About a year or so. And Cynthia is getting antsy," Loren said.

"That's so tragic."

For a moment, we didn't say anything more, until Loren said, "Anyway, let's get back to your goose." He shoved a stuffed ravioli in his mouth. "Listen," he said, cream sauce dribbling down his chin, "they want you in L.A. for the release of your book. There's a kid show out there that's taped and goes nationwide."

"Which one?" I stabbed at some radicchio.

"Kid Chat, Kid Talk, something like that. It's not offensive or clamorous where everyone gets dunked into some sort of shit. This is more highbrow, more PBSish."

I dabbed the cream sauce from his chin, but he didn't skip a beat.

"They have this segment where authors introduce their books, often read something from them. To whet the kids' appetites. They say this show's responsible for bouncing the sale of children's literature."

"I'd be working with a live audience? Of kids?"

He laughed. "That should scare the hell out of you."

I thought for a moment. "Not really. It's kind of exciting." Maybe I was actually going to get a piece of it. I could tell by the excitement in Loren's voice, he thought so, too. I rested my fork on my plate. "Thank you," I said.

He chewed and swallowed. "It's my job, Laura."

"Yeah, but you believed in me way back when Dad showed you that story I'd written when I was all of about fifteen." Another fifteen years passed since then, years of traveling through Europe, waitressing, going from boyfriend to boyfriend and shrink to shrink, all the while taking my lazy time to get through college. Once I was finally done, with a diploma to show for it, I didn't know where to go or what to do. That's when I saw an ad in a new publication called *Day's Notice* looking for writers. It took some convincing to have them hire a woman, but I managed to sell myself with a story I wrote on spec. The topic: where mothers take their children to play in Manhattan.

"Your dad was smart enough to see something there," Loren said, clasping a hand over mine. "I miss him, Laura. I miss him busting my chops about having moved off Long Island." He choked out the last sentence. "He saw your spark."

Spark. Funny, but I can still see my father fanning that spark into a raging blaze while Mom stands on the other side, pouring buckets of holy water on me to snuff it out. I want to scream, tell them to stop. But I don't. Instead, I just smolder.

From entrée to dessert, Loren discussed all the possibilities for my book before he finally said it was time he go find Esther. He paid the bill then stood and leaned over, kissing me on the forehead. "You let me know how your writing is coming along and how the house-hunting goes. If you need a co-signer...." He pointed to himself.

I thanked him with a smile and watched as he wove around some tables and disappeared out the door. I still had some coffee in my cup and decided to nurse it in quiet celebration.

Far as I'm concerned, Sunday mornings should be for sleeping. But this Sunday morning found me awake far too early. When I'd crawled between

the crisp sheets in the hotel room the night before, after having taken a lei-
surely bath, I'd looked forward to a long night's sleep, one that would take
a serious chunk out of the day. Almost immediately, I drifted off into delicious unconsciousness. To my dismay, however, at six a.m., as though my
body wasn't aware of the agreement I'd made with it hours earlier, my eyes
fluttered open. And no amount of punching my pillow and attempts at forcing my eyes to stay closed helped. The problem was that my mind kept playing back the previous evening's events.

Loren's words began to sink in. There was a very real possibility that my
book would actually make me financially secure, if there was such a thing.
Then, of course, there was the meeting of Peter—AKA Nancy Greenly. Our
paths crossing again wouldn't be so strange, since we were both represented
by the same literary agency. I just needed to figure out a way to get our paths
to cross again soon. It was too early to call Loren to find out if he could
somehow make it happen.

I gave up on the idea of sleep and jumped out of bed, pulling open the
curtains and letting light flood the room. I took a shower, applied some
mascara and blush, then slipped on a pair of jeans and white blouse. Not
much later, with key in hand, I scanned the room one last time to be sure
I'd left nothing behind, then let the door close behind me. Breakfast first,
then I'd call Loren. I strolled down the quiet corridor, my satchel draped
over my shoulder, and considered how I'd broach the topic of Peter Collins
without stirring Loren's curiosity. I reached the elevator and pressed the
down button.

It would have to be an insouciant call, one that wouldn't produce a ton
of questions.

The elevator swished open. It was empty, but with each consecutive
stop, more people began to pour in, pressing me closer to the back wall.

Another stop, another collective sigh.

"Don't s'pose there's any room for this bloke?" a voice said, with a familiar accent. "P'raps I should wait for the next lift."

I tried to see if it were Peter, but was squeezed in too tight. Calling out
his name would have sounded desperate. Once the elevator swept to the

lobby, the dam of people broke. I saw nothing but a blur of bodies, finding myself snagged in a dense, slow-moving crowd. I craned my neck to see over the mass of heads, but he was nowhere in sight; if he'd been there at all. Vanished like a vapor.

I shuffled to the check-out counter looking this way and that in hopes he was on the other side of a column or boxed into a cluster of hotel guests milling about. I handed over the key and decided I'd have to go back to plan A and call Loren after breakfast. I made my way over to the restaurant, waiting for the hostess to return from seating some patrons.

"Laura?"

I turned to find Peter standing behind me. With hasty contrived composure, I said, "Peter!"

"You alone?" He had a bulky newspaper folded under his arm.

"I wasn't up to the drive back last night, so I got a room," I said, while thinking *Plan B.*

"Oh," he said, scowling.

The hostess appeared. "Two?"

I looked at Peter, hoping he wasn't intent on reading his paper while sipping tea and wolfing down crumpets in solitary comfort. "Care to join me?" I said.

He hesitated, glancing at his paper. Finally, he said, "That would be fine."

We reached our table and Peter rested the paper next to him while I pushed my satchel under my chair. We sat down across from each other.

"So," I said, "did you have a nice dinner last night?"

He hummed a positive reply, then said, "Claire and Graham have been very decent to me. They originate from London, but have a flat here. They love spending their holidays in New York. Once Easter is over, they plan to return home and turn their flat over to me. For now, I'm staying here." He made a waving gesture toward the hotel. "And you?" he said.

I shot him a quizzical look.

"Last night I thought you said you were from New York," he said, a perceptible scowl on his forehead, "but you said you spent the night here."

"Oh! Yes, I recently went back to Long Island for awhile. Family issues. But I'll be moving back here shortly. After my meeting with Loren last night, it was just easier staying here."

The waitress took our beverage order and then invited us to check out the buffet.

"So, it sounds like you plan to stay in New York for awhile," I said.

He nodded. "I've been told by well-intentioned friends that I should get back in the swing of things. Claire and Graham validated that by offering me their flat for the summer."

I looked at the coffee and juice being placed before us, trying to hide any knowledge of his circumstance.

"I'm hoping this getaway will help," Peter said, giving an urgent rap to the table. He then took a deep breath and said, "S'pose we should see what fare they have to offer."

Soon we were in the midst of yeasty aromas. I wandered away from Peter and watched a chef who was cascading an egg mixture from a ladle onto a sizzling griddle. Another chef was slicing roast beef, au jus draining into the well of a cutting board, but I headed toward the gentler-looking wicker baskets filled with all sorts of muffins and breads. I put a blueberry muffin on my plate, heading back to the table to find Peter already seated.

"Is that all you're having?" he said, as I took my chair.

"Look who's talking." I nodded toward the solitary scone he was buttering.

"Rather daft, isn't it, being surrounded by all these tasty selections."

I smiled, but truth was, he was the first possibility who intrigued me for what I needed. The thought made me too nervous to eat.

He said, "So, what did Loren tell you about me?"

I purposely took a long sip of my coffee before replying. "What makes you think we talked about you?"

He shrugged. "Yes, I s'pose that was bloody presumptuous of me."

I leaned across the table. "Yes, both you *and* Nancy. She's quite a success."

"Ah, so he did mention that. Well, *she* certainly is. Well, was. Can't seem to get her to write another word, I'm afraid."

"I'm sorry, Peter. Loren also told me about your loss."

He took a drawn out sip of his tea, then placed his cup on the saucer, clinking the spoon against it as though absorbed by the tinging sound it made. He sighed, cleared his throat as if ready to speak, then took a harsh, fast bite of his scone.

I muttered, "I don't know what to say."

Keeping his eyes on his cup, he said, "I was hoping the change of scenery would inspire me to write, but after these few beastly days ... well, I'm not so sure anymore."

"Maybe you should write as Peter Collins, try a new genre."

"Funny, but I did mention that to Cynthia, but she wouldn't hear of it. People want Nancy Greenly. They haven't a clue who Peter Collins is."

"Screw Cynthia," I said. "You should write what's inspiring you."

He ran his hand through his hair. "That's the problem. Nothing's inspiring me at the moment. There's just no desire to put word to paper and I'm under contract to hand over another Nancy Greenly novel."

"Do you have children?"

He shook his head. "Cheryl scheduled our social affairs and I wrote. Children never played a part in that."

"Things'll get better," I said. "It takes time."

His face darkened. "Laura, it bloody well makes one angry when one is told the pain will stop." He leaned in, gazing into my eyes. "I don't want it to stop. That's all I have left of her."

I didn't respond nor could I imagine feeling that way. When my mother died, I felt the loss, but it was more from never having what could have been. As for my father, I hadn't quite broken through the resentment and bitterness I had toward him, but was working on it with my therapist.

Peter softened. "Sorry. Sometimes it's just a bit—"

"It's okay," I said. "I'm not very good at offering advice."

"And it's apparent I'm not good at taking it." He smiled. "We should get along famously." He leaned in. "I don't believe you told me what you write."

"Lots of things, but Loren represents my children's books."

The waitress dropped the check off at the table and Peter snatched it, signing his room number on it. I took out my wallet and tossed some bills on the table."

"Oh, that's how it is," he said.

"What's that mean?"

"You're a part of this women's movement."

I reached for my satchel. "It's just the tip," I said. We both stood and I said, "So, you have plans for the day?"

He paused, perhaps trying to come up with an escape.

"Listen," I said, "this isn't a come-on. I'm just not ready to go back to Long Island, yet."

"Well, I'm going to do some serious walking today, get to know New York a bit better."

"Oh," I said.

"Wouldn't mind your company, though."

"Do you think it's down there?" he said, haze swirling and wind rushing around us as we stood on the observation deck of the Empire State Building.

"Do I think what's down there?" I said.

"The plot. The next Nancy Greenly story."

"That's what you're looking for today?"

"A springboard, at least." He gazed out at the chunks of architecture, making it easier for me to survey him. His face wasn't hard, the type described in a Nancy Greenly novel as chiseled from granite. No, it was more like smooth sandstone, a slight angle here, another there; a face a finger could outline. And want to do it again.

"You'll find it, Peter," I said, my words lost in susurrus gusts.

He took my arm, leading the way back down. Soon we fell into the city's strolling Sunday rhythm until we came to a line wrapped around a building. We attached ourselves to the end and soon were pacing by a window display of a mechanical bunny hopping down a cottony trail, stopping every few feet at another robotic companion waiting with an Easter basket. With a rigid paw, the rabbit dropped in a purple and pink egg.

I strayed from the line, pressing my face against the window. A child wouldn't notice that the egg never left the bunny's paw; a child wouldn't see that the egg was plastic.

"Laura?"

I turned and saw Peter's curious expression.

"Is everything all right?"

It would be so brilliant to see the world through the eyes of a child. I nodded and followed Peter away from the crowd.

By the time we reached the hotel and I waited for the attendant to get my car, it was early Sunday evening. Peter said a polite good-bye, parting with my phone number tucked in his pocket. I was surprised he'd asked for it, but he said he wanted it so we could keep in touch. "No big deal," he said.

"No big deal," I replied before driving out of the parking garage.

CHAPTER FOUR

Jenny

No one really knows me, sometimes not even me. It's supposed to be enough to be a pastor's wife, but lately, it's not. I want something else, something more. And here I am once again on my knees, except this time I'm not in an attitude of prayer but leaning over a large, dilapidated cardboard box. I reached deep into it, groping assorted fragments of material and outdated patterns, hoping for something spring-like with Easter only days away. A few yards will be enough to sew together a blouse. What I pulled out is a piece of flannel designed with rattles, baby bottles and rocking horses, a remnant from a crib sheet set I'd made for Louise Hamilton's joyous occasion. I kept what was left in hopes of making something for my own baby.

I shoved it back to the bottom of the box and slumped onto the floor; if not a baby, then what? Sad to say, there's nothing else for me but to stand in the shadow of my husband's glory and his sister's persistent rays. That's not what truly bothers me, though. It's just I always figured I'd be a mother. Simple. I imagined sitting at the kitchen table helping my children with their homework. I pictured the four of us huddled together. We'd do projects, especially art. I'd show them how to draw.

But there is no children's laughter coming from our house and the kitchen table is free of any crayons and construction paper, and I'm left with knocking around the empty space looking for something to do, for some meaningful project—like sewing a blouse for Easter.

Don't get me wrong, I stay busy with church activities. But I yearn for the day when I can skip the meetings and the evening services, without needing an explanation. While Eric is across the street at the church preaching, I would be here at the parsonage rocking our baby to sleep. The thought that I may never get that maternal satisfaction sickens me.

In the beginning, when month after infertile month went by, I took it upon myself to go to the library for some books about the hushed subject. Where else could I go? I mean, the ladies from church hint at possible reasons why I'm not getting pregnant, but I cannot help wonder if they are dispensing silly old wives' tales. When I mentioned my concerns to my mother, she told me she'd pray for us. That was over two years ago. So, I have the prayers of the church and my mother working for me, but I'm beginning to think of it more like asking for bread and receiving a stone. Eric doesn't say anything, but he must wonder why I don't ask God for a baby anymore.

I never demanded too much of Eric, but after scouring the books at the library and discovering some easy, mind-boggling solutions, I asked him to switch from his briefs to roomy boxer shorts. He was willing to try, but after several months of giving his sperm a chance to spring to life and nothing happened—even after we conscientiously did it during my supposed fertile time—I made an appointment with a specialist.

Medicine isn't cheap, though, especially with our meager insurance plan. Still, I dipped into our grocery money, living on beans and rice most of the time, which isn't such a big deal when you've been a missionary kid. But I'm willing to sacrifice anything to get a baby, even my pride.

Growing up in the Philippines, medical care was minimal. Check-ups consisted of a doctor peering into my ears, nose and eyes, and a few uncomfortable moments while he rested the stethoscope on my just-forming breasts. But once Eric and I decided to find out why I wasn't getting pregnant, I yielded to the healing science and put my self-respect aside.

The doctor saw parts of me I never dared to explore. He analyzed blood and urine samples, had me take my temperature every morning and chart it. Once the tests were complete, he said nothing appeared out of order—there was no medical explanation for my not getting pregnant. That's the moment my heart became hardened toward God. It was as if He decided I was not worthy of being a mother. But then the doctor continued and said, not as long as sperm was reaching my egg. "Matter of fact," he said, "I suggest Mr. Sumner see his doctor."

Eric was seated beside me and mumbled, "Please call me Pastor Sumner."

"My apologies," the doctor said, tapping his pen on the folder in front of him, looking from me to Eric, waiting.

I couldn't bear to look at Eric, certain I'd see a face rigid with propriety. I held my breath, expecting him to proselytize the doctor about God's *new* will, which required that our condition be left in His hands, and not man's—doctor or not.

Instead, breaking the silence, his voice soft and steady, he asked the doctor what he needed to do. Tears welled in my eyes. I wondered if his mother were still alive if he would have been so opened to try something beyond prayer. He's told me in bitter bits and painful pieces how unyielding his mother had been, but I must say that since she was put deep into the ground, he's changed, become more relaxed. That day in the doctor's office, I witnessed a man who seemed less fearful. I fell in love with him all the more.

Sitting on the cold, tile floor, leaning against the caved-in box of material, I couldn't help but smile recalling Eric acting as if he were comfortable with what he was doing. He'd strolled down the hall at the clinic, leaving me in the waiting room blindly leafing through magazines, wondering how he would spill his semen for testing.

I turned the pages to *McCalls, Redbook* and several issues of other magazines I had little interest in before he emerged. He refused to make eye contact with me and at his side, discreet in his hand, was the container.

"Oh, you could've left that in the room," the nurse at the desk said. His face red, he turned to bring it back, but she called out to him, "Reverend Sumner!" He stopped, looking over at her, attempting to hide the container. "No need to go for a second round. One should be enough." She motioned for him to approach the desk.

I was the only one left in the waiting room, but he found the incident mortifying and it took some time to calm him down. However, by that evening we were able to laugh about it, me more than him.

Then, with sober anxiety, we were left to wait for the results.

A week later, sitting on the edge of our chairs, we were told the news was not bad: Eric's sperm appeared plentiful and eager. Without offering any solution, the doctor dismissed us with an assuring smile, handshake and comment: "Just go about your daily lives and perhaps you'll soon have a pleasant surprise."

"But there has to be something more that we can do," I said.

"There are drugs," he said. "But...."

"But what?" Eric said.

"Well, they're rather costly and then there's the chance of multiple births."

Eric and I looked at each other, mentally rolling over what the doctor was saying.

"Listen," the doctor said, "oftentimes stress can be the cause. Try to relax and perhaps that'll be the answer."

No sooner did we walk out of the office did I begin to sob. Where was the practical solution, the answer to my prayers?

"God's testing you," Beth had said a couple of weeks ago on the Sunday Laura made her announcement. "He wants to see if you trust Him."

Then after one of our prayer meetings, old Mrs. Tregette shuffled over to me and grasped my hand. "Maybe you're not meant to have children, dear. Not everyone is."

Then why, if I'm not supposed to have any, do I want them so badly?

That barren nagging sank into me again and I pushed myself from the floor, leaving material piled around the box. I went to the window and leaned on the sill. Across the street, standing white, pristine, a beacon in a spiritually starved community was Seabrook Evangelical Church. My church. A prodding billboard promised: *We have what you're looking for!*

"How ya doing, hon?"

I jumped, startled by Eric's sudden appearance. I rushed to the scattered material and gathered it, shoving it back in the box. "I was trying to come up with something for Sunday," I said.

"Wish I could buy you a new Easter dress," Eric said, grasping my arm, pulling me to him. "And a hat."

I placed my hand on my head. "Like some high society woman?"

"Mmm." He pressed me against him, nuzzling my neck. "Why don't you take a break?"

I once melted in his arms when he held me the way he was doing now, but sex has become something else, mocking me month after month, reminding me that I failed yet again.

"It's in the middle of the afternoon," I said.

"I know that." He lifted a strand of my hair, smelling it.

"Well, what if someone comes to the door?"

"We don't answer it."

"Yeah right," I said, feeling how much he wanted me. I have to admit that it's been some time, with me dodging his advances. This time, though, he was more persistent and I let him lead me across the hall to the bedroom. Not much later, our worn out chenille bedspread was all that covered us. I tried to respond to his kisses, but found his intensity distracting as he forced himself inside me. He was more determined than loving, his rhythm frantic. The more he worked to gain entrance, the more I tensed, fighting him in a clinch. Wave after nauseating wave, he crashed over me, on me, in me. I fought back without meaning to until I closed my eyes, attempting to succumb.

Finally, he groaned and rolled off me. Between gasps, he kept saying he was sorry.

A tear escaped and I tried to brush it away before he saw it. "I'm okay," I said.

He sighed in exasperation, covering his face with his hands. "*Okay?* Remember when it was more than *okay?* Remember when we actually enjoyed each other?"

The telephone rang and instead of letting it continue to ring, he grabbed it.

I lay motionless, grateful I didn't have to respond to what he said. By the sound of the one-way conversation it wasn't a serious call, but just an inquiry about buying an Easter lily for service. I decided to get up and slid out from under the covers, but Eric reached out to me. The phone to his ear, he looked at me, smiling his forgive-me smile. He began caressing my back, working my muscles. I didn't resist. I didn't want to anymore. I wanted that melting feeling again, to love him again and let that be enough.

He slid an arm around me, his fingers gliding down, then further down. I turned to him, covering him with my body. I kissed his chest, using my hands the way I used to when I first explored him.

"It'll be done, Mrs. Chase," he said. "Thanks for calling." He started to hang up, then added: "That's right. Yup, should be."

He was ready for me again and I shifted so that we became one. The phone slipped from his grasp, his eyes rolling. I stifled a laugh.

"Sure thing," he said. "Okay, see you Sunday. Thanks, I will." At last, he hung up. "Mrs. Chase sends her love." He cupped his hand on the back of my head, bringing my face to his. "Think I'll give you mine instead."

I sank into what can only be described as pleasure, easing into love-making with an ache for satisfaction. I wrapped my legs around his ropy limbs. He brought me to him, on him. It used to be more than physical for me. There'd been a time it was spiritual, lifting me to a heavenly place. And that's where it carried me now as I gripped Eric with all my intensity.

"Savor it, Jen," he whispered to my moans, taking me by the hips and bringing me to him over and over again.

I didn't want it to end. If I could have drawn him into my soul, I would have and I wasn't about to let him go while I soared. And soar, I did. I couldn't stop if I wanted to.

Finally, breathlessly, I collapsed in his hold. It had been too long a wait, too frustrating. Too demanding. But not today. Today had been a release.

We lay quietly, with me resting in his arms. He lifted strands of my hair, bringing them to his face. Eventually, he spoke.

"I think I'll go over and talk to Beth later."

I leaned on my elbow, looking him in the eye. "About?"

"Selling the house."

"She hates talking about it."

"We need the money, Jen. We have every right to it. This way we could buy our own place."

Living in the parsonage meant we didn't have to worry about a mortgage or rent, but it also meant we weren't considered established enough to adopt.

"You really think we could buy our own place?" I said.

He rubbed my shoulder. "It won't be a mansion, Jen, but Dad paid next to nothing for that house years ago. We'll get a nice amount, even split three ways."

I fell back into his arms. It crossed my mind to suggest he should wait until after Easter before broaching the subject with Beth, but that would mean time wasted.

He said, "Remember that mint green dress you wore to your parents' anniversary party?"

I nodded.

"Looks nice on you."

Later that afternoon, I went back to my sewing room and pushed the box back into the corner.

Laura

"Just let it ring a few more times, please." I stood in the hallway, the phone cradled to my shoulder, while trying to work a stubborn earring into the hole in my ear.

Please pick up, Peter. I stretched the cord as far as it would go, while attempting to get my foot in my leather beige pump, which was just out of reach.

"Ma'am," the hotel operator cut in, "if Mr. Collins hasn't picked up by now, he must be out."

"He could be in the shower," I said, as the phone crashed from the pine stand to the floor. I rushed to pick it up. "Hello? Hello?"

"I'm here," the operator replied with little enthusiasm.

"Just let it ring a few more times. Please."

Late the night before I discovered a note written in Beth's scribble on my dresser, saying that "a Peter" had called. I couldn't be sure how long the laconic message had been on my dresser, but it demanded my attention.

"Ma'am, please...."

"Okay, okay," I said. "I'll try again later."

I hung up and raced back to the bedroom, slipping on my shoes, then took a hasty glance at myself in the mirror. I'd chosen a matching silk blazer and skirt set, the color of a robin's egg, for Easter service. I couldn't believe I was putting myself through the ordeal. I had little intention of doing so, but earlier in the week Eric had stopped by looking for Beth.

"She's at the grocery store," I'd said.

He walked into the living room. "I was hoping to talk to her about the house."

"Good luck."

"So, I hear you're coming to Easter dinner."

I nodded, wishing I had a good enough excuse not to.

"Maybe you'd consider coming to service first."

"Eric...."

"It's just you never heard me preach before." When he saw my expression of warning, he cut himself short and said, "Whatever you want to do. No pressure." He walked to the front door and before leaving, said, "No need to tell Beth I was by. I'll catch up with her later."

I think it was the first time he'd ever asked me to do much of anything for him, which explains why I'm up and dressed in my Sunday best at such an ungodly hour. But, I find it difficult to believe it will be him standing up at that altar. He's my brother. I know his shortcomings all too well. Besides, it's the same church where I grew up watching Pastor Allen do a peacock strut, bugling how we were all damned to hell.

Beth left hours earlier to teach Sunday school and if I didn't get in gear, I'd be stuck in the back of the church sitting on a folding chair.

I grabbed my purse and ran downstairs, remembering my mother by singing one of her favorite hymns: "Onward Christian soldier, marching as to war."

And I'm off to the battlefield of my youth.

The foyer was quiet, except for the drone of the organ beyond the closed doors. Service had begun and I was late. A gray-haired man with sagging jowls approached me. "Happy Easter, Laura."

I nodded in response, but couldn't figure out how he knew my name.

"Don Simpson," he said, shaking my hand. "Head deacon."

Another nod, but this time with a forced smile.

"I helped officiate at your father's...."

"Of course," I said, still not recognizing him, but the name was familiar.

"I'll be seeing you at your brother's today, for dinner."

That's right! It had been Jenny's mere mention of his name that made Beth tremble. "Sorry I'm late," I said.

"Never too late," he said, taking my elbow and leading me to the closed double doors. He opened them and, instantly, an aromatic blast of lilies and every other possible perfume rushed at me. With Don's guidance, I swam through the fragrance, not stopping until we reached the first row. Beth looked up, tears springing to her eyes. She shifted closer to Jenny, her thickset body quivering like a bowl of yesterday's Jell-O, and patted the created space next to her. I thought Don was going to follow me, but he walked up to the altar to join Eric. I squeezed in next to Beth and in a whisper told her not to get all soppy or I'd leave.

The low tone of the organ suddenly burst into a loud rendition of "He's Alive!" and the congregation rose; in Pavlovian fashion, so did I. Eric makes eye contact with me and nods appreciatively. He is singing the hymn with as much passion as he once sang "Hound Dog." He used to pretend he was Elvis, but a hushed Elvis behind his closed bedroom door so that our mother couldn't see him grinding his hips or hear him singing the devil's words.

After the hymn ended, Don strolled over to the lectern. "Let us pray," he said, and thanked God for creating so beautiful a day to celebrate history's most important event. Out of the corner of my eye, I saw that Beth was rubbing her arms while watching the deacon with wide-eyed attention.

Once the offering was collected and another hymn sung, Deacon Don surrendered the lectern to Eric.

My brother the pastor, his chest swelling, exploded, "My, it's good to be in the house of the Lord today!" His joyful outburst inspired a rousing "Amen!" from the congregation. He warmed the flock with a humorous story, earning him a chuckle or two before he opened the Bible, taking on a solemn expression.

He read from the Book of Acts, then said, "It was with great faith, these men, these apostles, went out to preach the good news to the world." He lifted his Bible for verification. "This was a corrupt world, one not eager to hear the error of its ways. Much like today, much like our neighbors."

Beth's perennial permed head bobbed in agreement.

"But, we must learn to expurgate our sinful nature and take on a new spirit, a spirit filled with abounding joy."

Someone behind me said, "Amen!"

"This is what the Resurrection is all about. Abounding joy. Not death, but life!"

More scattered "Amens" came from the congregation.

"Now," he said, "please turn to Luke twenty-four with me."

Riffling pages filled the sanctuary. Beth brought her Bible closer so we could share, but I found that my thoughts were beginning to wander, much like when I was a child. Besides, I could have preached the sermon myself. Verbatim. Maybe that was why Eric was up there. Living this life means little challenge. It's a role he can play.

Other than the fact that it was Eric up on the altar and not Pastor Allen, nothing had really changed since I'd stopped coming all those years ago. The austere sanctuary has been kept the same. There's the picture of Jesus over the choir loft, his sorrowful eyes gazing heavenward. And there, by the window, was the Ten Commandments carved not in stone but a thick oak plank. I used to try to tune out Pastor Allen's melodramatic hoopla by seeing if I could rattle off each commandment in my head, preparing to challenge Beth, as futile as that could be. I once knew them by heart, but do I still? I lowered my eyes and tested myself.

One by one, I mentally scrolled through each, making it all the way to the ninth: *Thou shalt not bear false witness against thy neighbor.* The verse hit me like an electric bolt, causing Beth and Jenny to look at me with startled expressions. Even Eric paused for a moment, glancing down at me. I tried to gather myself, taking a tissue from my pocketbook and dabbing at the perspiration on my face. I then tried to reach the finish line of the tenth commandment, but could not make it beyond the ninth. I was regressing to a time that had been buried deep in my psyche and could do nothing to stop it. Why had no amount of therapy unearthed it? Now it surfaced, rushing through my every pore. I longed for Dr. Davis to help me, but since she was nowhere nearby and I was unable to escape the memory, I rolled back in time:

I was popping a pimple on my forehead, when my mother called from the bottom of the stairs, "Laura! What are you doing? Get down here and set the table!"

I hurriedly turned down my stereo, even though the volume was barely audible, and ran out into the hallway. "Be right down." I went back into my room and lifted the needle from *Come On-a My House*. I took the record off the turntable and slipped it into the sleeve of my Word Choir album, keeping Rosemary Clooney from my mother's shrewd eye, and then ran downstairs to the kitchen.

"What were you doing up there?" Mother said.

"Homework." I pulled the dishes out of the cabinet and began setting the table, knowing my mother was studying me. She said, "Well, I have some news."

I knew that was an ominous statement, but didn't bother pressing her, since she had her own sense of timing. Moments later, Dad dawdled in from the backyard with Eric behind him. Just as the meatloaf was placed on the table, Beth wandered in and we all sat down, bowing our heads. Mom had Eric ask the blessing. Once he was finished and before I had a chance to scoop some macaroni on to my plate, Mom said, "You have an appointment with Pastor Allen this Saturday."

I looked up to see that she was addressing me. "What?"

"You heard me," she said.

Beth's voice was low, tremulous, when she said, "Why are you having her go to him?"

"Well," Mom said, passing the meatloaf to my father, "your sister is at a very crucial point in her life. At fourteen, she needs spiritual guidance."

I glanced at Dad, watching him chew his supper, slow and meticulous.

My mother continued her explanation. "Pastor will be able to explain why that music she is so desperate to listen to is the devil's music."

"Why don't *you* tell me, Mom?" I said.

"He'll also tell you why it's so dangerous to be boy crazy at your age."

"I'm not boy crazy," I said. There was just one boy, John Blakely, a junior I couldn't stop thinking about, but I was sure he didn't even know my name.

"And, just so you know, we decided you see him on a weekly basis."

"We?" I said, looking at my father.

"Not your father," Mom said. My father looked across the table at Mom while she said, "HE'S chosen to pass as the spiritual leader in this house."

My father's plate was still full, but without saying a word, he got up, bringing it to the sink, and walked out into the backyard.

"Pastor Allen and I," Mom said. "*We* decided."

"Mom," Beth said, her bottom lip quivering, "does she really need to go? I'll help her."

"You!" I yelled.

"Laura," Mom said, "do not raise your voice in this house. And, Beth, it's better Laura have the Pastor's wisdom. True, if it wasn't for Pastor Allen, you wouldn't be in charge of the youth group and wouldn't have had the chance to go to Kansas. But Laura needs someone with a firmer hand."

Beth sat motionless, her eyes transfixed on her plate.

I said, "I'm not going." Belt or no belt, I meant it.

"Well, that's where you're wrong, young lady," Mom said, with just as much conviction.

I rose from the table and brought my plate to the sink. I looked out the window into the backyard where my father was practicing his golf swing. Beth came up alongside of me, placing her dish on the counter. It was her turn to wash. She turned on the faucet and took out the box of Dreft from under the sink. She started to pour some powder into the rushing water, but then whirled around and dashed into the bathroom. I turned off the faucet.

Eric remained at the table, taking a second helping.

Choking noises came from the bathroom, followed by the sound of Beth's dinner splashing into the toilet.

So it was.

On Saturday morning at ten o'clock I had my first meeting with Pastor Allen at his office, which was tucked away in the back of the church. It was obvious that Mom had prearranged an agreement with him so that I didn't duck out of the meetings. She pulled up in the front of the church and gave her horn a toot. The door swung open with him standing there. Once I entered, after dawdling up the walkway, he waved my mother on her way for the hour.

At that first meeting, I purposely wore dungarees, instead of the appropriate dress for the 1950s. I wanted to be shock-inducing and rebellious, imitate the scandalous fashion photos of women wearing pants. It had been only a few weeks from when Pastor had preached against women trying to look like men, but he didn't seem angry with me that afternoon. Instead, he made me feel uneasy with the way his rheumy eyes did a slow dance down my girlish body. The following week I was back wearing a long skirt and blouse buttoned up to my neck. However, it was as if the white-haired man was looking right through my clothes while he talked to me about God.

"Laura, dear," he said, "you must know the awful time you're giving your mom." He sat perched in front of me on his desk.

I kept my eyes down, my hands folded on my lap, counting the minutes for the session to be over.

"She cares about your walk with Jesus. She cares about *you*."

I wondered if I showed him the welts on my legs, if he would still believe she cared.

He hopped from the desk and crouched before me, his damp, doughy hands on mine. "She loves you, Laura. The Lord loves you." He paused, sucked up some air, then said, "And, of course, I love you."

I pulled my hands away, realizing too late the mistake I made. Now his hands were free to rest on my legs, the cotton of my skirt feeling much too thin.

"I wanna go home."

"Why, we've a good forty minutes left." His thumbs caressed my thighs. "The way I see it, I could be a very big help to you, Laura. You just might get to keep listening to that music you so dearly love…with your mother's blessings." His face, beaded with sweat, was inches from mine.

"See?" he said. "I bet you didn't think it'd be like this." His words came faster. "Like I'm trying to tell you, we all love you." He hesitated, looked to be struggling for just the right words. "And, you know, Laura, love has so many angles, nuances. Do you know what that word means?"

"I wanna call my house," I said, my eyes cast downward. "I don't feel good." But it was as if Pastor didn't hear me.

He brought his clasped hands to his chin. "But you're a smart girl and first you must show me how much you love me. We need to trust each other.

Then I bet we could talk your mother into comin' round a little bit to your side."

He started breathing funny, his breath warm on my face.

"Remember last week you read about Mary washing Jesus' feet with her hair?" He reached out, running his hand through my pony tail. I pressed as far back in my chair as I could, but it wasn't far enough. "You don't have to do that for me, of course." He laughed. "But what do you think that verse teaches?"

I began to tremble, tears filling my eyes. My throat was too tight to speak.

"Don't know?" he said. "See, that's why you're here, for me to teach you." He pulled me to him, smothering me. "What that verse teaches, Laura, is how willing Mary was to please her Lord. How she wanted to obey authority."

I pushed away, but his thick hands found my legs again and he began rubbing them, squeezing them.

"And Mary was rewarded for pleasing Jesus. It's a lesson we must learn: How to obey and please without asking questions."

He slid his hands higher up my thighs and I pushed away as hard as I could, causing the leg of the chair to catch on the carpet, tipping me over. I landed hard on the floor, the wind knocked out of me, my skirt hiked above my knees. I tried to push it down, but Pastor's hands got there first.

It was an hour that lasted days, and when the long-awaited horn beeped, I raced down the sidewalk to mother's car. I didn't turn to look, but I knew Pastor was returning my mother's cheerful wave.

I scrambled in the car, slammed the door shut and locked it. For the first time I could remember, I was grateful to have my mother nearby.

"How'd it go?" she said, pulling the car into the street.

I shrugged, staring at the houses, all the same shape and style, whirring by.

"Laura, I'm talking to you."

My mouth was dry. I didn't know if I could talk and sure enough began to cry. I couldn't help it. Between sobs, I begged her not to send me back to him.

"I don't think two weeks has helped the likes of you."

My fear began to turn into anger. I said, "I'm not going back."

"What did you say?"

"I'm not going back." The tears had stopped.

"Obviously, you need more lessons on respect, not to mention obedience. You are going back, young lady."

"Please, Mom, I can't." I couldn't stop thinking about how his hands groped me, fondled me, reached inside me, probing—all the while with me fighting with fists that were useless, screams that were muffled. "He makes me feel funny."

"That's the spirit of God."

"No, Mom, it's not," I said, screaming. "He touched me!"

My mother lifted her foot from the gas pedal and the car behind screeched and blared, then swerved around us, the driver giving us a nasty gesture. She gaped at me. "What are you saying?"

I spilled the entire story, how Pastor Allen touched me, how he tried to make me touch him and how I refused. I was quick to ease my mother's worry and told her he hadn't gone all the way. *All the way*, a phrase my friends and I whisper among ourselves, something I would do in a heartbeat if John Blakely asked me.

Without another word between us, my mother made a U-turn. Her expression was set as she drove back to the church. I was tempted to scoot over and sit by her, but we reached the church before I dared to budge.

"Come with me," she said, lunging from the car. I trailed behind her, amazed at how enraged she'd become toward a man she revered as long as I could recall. *Where would we go to worship now?* We reached the office and a smiling, composed Pastor Allen opened the door, a Bible spread open in his large, roaming hands. I stood behind my mother until she made me come forward.

"Tell him what you just told me." Her face was flushed to purple.

I stuttered, noticing the chair was in its rightful spot. Papers that had been scattered all over the floor were stacked neatly on his desk next to his phone that I knocked down when I attempted to reach it. The white wisps of Pastor's hair were swept neatly in place, his trousers zipped.

"What's that, Laura?" He gazed kindly at me, a faint smile on his placid face.

I hesitated at first, but then did it. I blurted the whole store, how he'd unzipped himself, fondled himself when I wouldn't. I showed my mother the button that popped off my blouse in the struggle.

"So," my mother said, "you see my problem." She sidled up alongside of Pastor.

He snapped his Bible shut and placed a hand on my mother's shoulder, his smile melting into an expression of pity. "It's clear to me what she's trying to do," he said. "And she certainly does have an overactive, debased imagination. Perhaps it is that music that gives her these horrid, horrid ideas."

I stared at him. "You made me promises. You…you told me if I did what you asked me to do—"

"Laura!" my mother screamed. "Enough."

"I must admit, Elizabeth," he said, "you do have your hands full with this one. When you told me how difficult she is, why I thought perhaps you were having typical teenage problems."

"I don't know, maybe we should send her to that retreat."

Pastor shook his head. "Elizabeth, I'd love to but they can only take a number of girls each year." He coughed, seemed to be grasping for words. "I don't think I could ask them again so soon."

I stood by watching my life being discussed.

"But, it did wonders for Beth. Maybe if I wrote a letter."

Pastor retorted, "It'd be a waste of time!" He turned toward me, blocking my mother's view. "I could've helped you. We could've been friends."

"Laura, tell Pastor you're sorry."

"I'm not lying!" I said.

Pastor turned to my mother. "That's right," he said.

I gasped, grateful for the sudden redemption, but then he added, "It's the devil living inside her. And it's your job, Elizabeth, to correct that."

My mother stared at me, her jaw tight. "Tell him now that you're sorry."

When I refused, my mother latched onto my ponytail and yanked me out of the office. I begged for her to believe me during the car ride home, but the only response I got was her heavy breathing. As soon as we got home, she marched to the closet and pulled the belt off the nail, ordering me upstairs to my room.

"What on earth is the matter now?" my father said, meeting us on his way downstairs.

"Why don't you ever stop her?" I cried. "Why do you let her—?"

Mother nudged me up the steps. "It's no concern to your father."

"Elizabeth," he said, "do you really need to do that?"

She stopped, facing him. "Yes, I do."

"She's a kid, Elizabeth. They make mistakes."

"Mistakes? *You* should know about mistakes."

Dad's face went white. "Don't punish her for mine."

"Oh, don't worry; she's making enough on her own."

He said nothing more, but trudged down the steps, abandoning me yet again.

When I reached the landing, Beth opened her bedroom door and gazed at me. "What'd he do?" she said. At first I thought she meant our father, but then she added: "Did he tell you he loved you, too?"

Before I could answer, my mother pushed me into my room. "The Ninth Commandment warns us not to bear false witness against our neighbor." She slammed the bedroom door. "What you tried to do to a godly man like Pastor Allen must be punished. Do you understand what accusations like that can do to a man's reputation?"

She wrapped the end of the belt around her hand. "I just praise God He gives me the wisdom to see through your little ploys. 'Thou givest thy mouth to evil, and thy tongue frameth deceit.' Now lift your blouse."

There was no escape. I obeyed, lifting my blouse.

A loud crack jerked me back to the present. I looked up toward the altar to see that Eric had dropped his Bible on the lectern for effect.

"We must claim our faith," he said. "Not hide it, but let it shine so that no darkness … no matter how deep … can overpower it." He lowered his voice. "Let us close in prayer."

Everyone bowed their heads. Except me. The whipping had been the worst ever. I wasn't able to sleep on my back for days. Then after, my mother ransacked my room, pulling out my dresser drawers, searching for more proof that I was the devil's own. She didn't find my Rosemary Clooney album tucked in the sleeve of the Christian album cover, but she did find my diary and demanded I give her the key. She questioned who J.B. was and told me if I kept it up, I'd find myself in trouble. She then told me that she wasn't going to waste Pastor Allen's time with me any longer. I was her problem and her problem only.

However, the image now that kept coming back to me was Beth standing in the hallway asking if Pastor Allen told me he loved me, too. *Too?*

While Eric prayed, I reached for Beth's hand and held it. She looked confused, but kept a tight hold until Eric said Amen and dismissed the congregation. But the epiphany immediately got lost in the hub of activity. I told Beth I had to get to the bakery before heading over to Eric and Jenny's.

"Wait," she said. "I want to see if you recognize someone." She led me across the aisle toward a hunched old woman who was leaning on a cane.

"Mrs. Tregette," Beth said, "you remember my sister, Laura, don't you?"

The woman reached out to me, leaving me little choice but to give her a hug. Her skin was so loose that it shifted at my touch. I imagined her bones were brittle enough they'd break at contact. I did recognize her, though. She was my Sunday school teacher years ago. Even then, she seemed ancient. Now she was just a ruin.

"Oh, my goodness," she said, her head bobbing involuntarily. Her sunken eyes brightened only to retract into corrugated wrinkles, and she kept wincing.

"Are you all right?" I said.

Her grimace faded. "I just wish the good Lord would see fit to take me home. I've been ready for years." She squeezed my hand with cold thin fingers. "Maybe I'm supposed to be right here, right now, though, letting you know how much your mother wanted to see you through those pearly gates."

"Oh, she let me know," I said, backing away.

"Laura!" Beth said, staring at me.

"I have to get to the bakery," I said. Mrs. Tregette looked confused.

"Oh," Beth said, "that's not necessary. I baked some pies."

"But I promised Jenny," I said, leaving Beth standing with Mrs. Tregette. I pushed through a chatty cluster of women, trying not to brush up against them, as if their floral dresses might be contaminated with poison ivy. It was all so reminiscent of my childhood, a straight and narrow path littered with a haunted past and I wanted nothing to do with it.

The gentle warmth of the morning sun grew into a sweltering afternoon heat, pressing on me as I hauled the desserts from my car. For each box I rested on the hood of the Thunderbird, a child stood in the next yard scrutinizing me.

"Whoa, Laura, there's just the five of us!" Eric appeared, taking the boxes by their strings. He'd changed from his blue suit to a yellow polo shirt and pair of jeans.

"You lose weight?" I said, noticing his diminishing paunch.

"If I did, I'll put it all back on today." He nodded at the stack of boxes.

"Everything looked so good, I couldn't decide."

"Happy Easter, Rich," Eric called over to the next yard. "How's it going?"

"Can't complain." The lanky neighbor ambled over, eyeing my car. "59, ain't it?"

I nodded, aware of the children still inspecting me.

Eric introduced me to Rich, but he was more interested in the car. "It's a beauty, isn't it?" Eric said. "Someday she's going to give it to me." He gave me a nudge, smiling.

"Mint condition," Rich said touching the fender.

I left the men talking about the car, a car I had no intention of buying when I stumbled on it at a bitter divorcée's garage sale. She, the divorcée, looked at the car as an albatross and sold it to me for next to nothing. I grabbed one of the boxes and walked over to the children. Three smudged faces cautiously watched me.

"Here," I said, handing the box over to one little boy. "Cookies. For you to share."

I was rewarded with a toothless grin before he was surrounded by the other children tearing into the box. I turned to help Eric carry the rest of the desserts into the kitchen. We were greeted by steaming pots rattling on the stove. The table was cluttered with empty bowls waiting to be filled, stacked utensils and a Bible splayed open as if tossed in a rush. Jenny came in from the living room, her face flushed, her hair clipped up into a bun. She had the mint green dress on she'd worn to church, except now there was a red apron over it.

"More dessert?" she said, her eyes growing wide.

That's when I noticed a long line of pies on the counter. Pies heaped with meringue, some lattice topped and others sealed and fluted to perfection; Beth's pies.

She walked into the kitchen and I said, "When did you bake these?"

"At night," she said. "You were working late a lot this week."

"Hey, Laura," Don said, walking in from the living room. "Your sister certainly outdid herself, didn't she?"

"Yes, she did," I said.

Beth waved us off, her face turning red. That's when it occurred to me that the pies may have been more for Don's benefit than for any other reason.

Not much later we were all seated around the cumbrous table that filled most of the space in the makeshift dining area in the corner of the living room. Deacon Don did the honors of asking the blessing. During the meal, I saw how Beth barely put any food on her plate, how her hand had a nervous tremble. She was behaving like a young girl and I ached for her just then. A woman in her thirties shouldn't be so inexperienced.

"That's a very pretty dress, Beth," I said. "Is it new?"

She looked up at me, her expression irritated. "New? I haven't bought anything new in ages, Laura."

Jenny passed the platter of sliced ham to Don, inviting him to take seconds.

"Oh," I said. "It's just I don't recognize it."

"Why would you?" she said, her voice tight. "But I don't have the money to buy anything new."

"Beth," Eric said, "I don't think Laura is questioning your finances. She was just complimenting your dress."

"Is that what you thought?" I said. Besides, my determination in having the house sold would now be more for Eric and Jenny's benefit than mine, since by Loren's account my book deal was going to be lucrative.

"Well," Don said, "I recognize it and it's always been a favorite of mine."

Beth's face was as red as the pickled beets that Eric was scooping onto his plate. "Thank you," she mumbled.

"Helen never seemed to buy a ham that wasn't salty," Don said. "This is delicious." He shoved a piece in his mouth.

"You must miss her," Jenny said. She then turned to me, her voice low and somber. "Don's wife was killed about a year ago. So tragic."

"Oh, goodness," I said. "I'm so sorry, Don. How'd it happen?"

"Car accident," he said.

Peter came to mind just then. I wondered what he was doing. I was eager to get home to try and call him again. Once it appeared everyone had taken their last bite, I began clearing the table.

"I'll get the dessert on," Jenny said.

"Let me help," Beth said.

"And I'll do these dishes," I said. I went into the kitchen and filled the sink with water and liquid soap, stopping for a moment to hand Eric a towel.

"What's this for?" he said.

"It's a new era, brother. You can dry."

"Well, let me help, too," Don said, grabbing a towel from the counter.

While I began washing dishes, Beth and Jenny took trips from the kitchen to the dining area, carrying pies and the desserts I'd brought. Coffee was percolating on the stove.

"Come on, Sis," Eric said, "you're going way too slow." I caught him winking at Don.

"Yeah," Don said, "looks like we're too fast for you."

"Really?" I said.

"Yeah," Eric said, "and I think you missed a spot. Better redo this one." Eric put a clean plate back into the sink.

Without hesitation, I scooped up some bubbles and slathered him in the face. With an evil chuckle, he twisted the damp dish towel and snapped it within inches from my backside.

"Don't you dare!" I squealed, skipping out of range.

When Jenny reached for the dessert plates in the cabinet, Eric dabbed bubbles on the tip of her nose. In a flash, she ran to the sink and scooped up a handful and tried to dump them on his head. In his attempt to dodge her, he slipped, landing on the floor.

"Oh no!" he said, grabbing Jenny's legs, pulling her down on to the floor with him. She screamed for help, so I held him down while she rubbed soap in his hair.

What we were doing just then, laughing loud and raucous, made my coming to Easter dinner worth it. The free-spirited Eric was the brother I recalled. Well, free-spirited when Mom wasn't around. I felt like eight years old again.

"You're all a bunch of kids," Beth said, shaking her head and darting around our entangled bodies. As she was reaching for the coffee cups, a dish towel snapped her on the behind. She wheeled around, her eyes wide. There stood Don, the weapon draped in his hand.

"Deacon Don!"

There was a collective giggle coming from the three of us piled on top of each other, looking up.

"Don," he said. "My name's Don, Beth."

She put the coffee cups on the counter and took off down the hall, slamming the bathroom door.

"Just isn't used to horseplay," Eric said. We all stood and straightened ourselves.

"Maybe I should leave," Don said.

"No!" Jenny and I said in unison.

"I need help eating all the dessert, Don," Eric said.

By the time Beth reappeared, the coffee was poured. "Sorry I offended you," Don said, holding out a chair for her.

She fluttered her arms and murmured that his apology was accepted, then hastily asked who was up for some pie. Don picked up his plate and asked for a slice of coconut cream. Once he took a bite, he said, "Ever think of opening up your own bakery?" Beth blushed and pooh-poohed him, but I saw a trace of a smile.

After an appropriate space of time passed between dessert and more small talk, I got up to leave, insisting that I could let myself out. I hesitated in the kitchen. Earlier, at service, when the basket was passed for donations, I handed it over to Beth without putting in a dime. Now, I pulled out a wad of bills from my purse and tucked them in a juice glass in the cabinet before leaving.

Later, after trying Peter again without reaching him, I attempted to work on my next installment of the *Pink Goose*, but couldn't get the memory of Beth's question out of my mind.

Did he tell you he loved you, too?

The paper in my typewriter remained blank. I decided to get a soda and went down to the kitchen. Earlier, when I'd gone upstairs, it was daylight and there was no need to turn on a light, but now it was past nine and everything was immersed in darkness. I got my soda, then went outside and sat on the front stoop. The neighborhood was quiet. It seemed there were no more children on the block. Most of us had moved away, I supposed. I closed my eyes, a memory washing over me.

"Why don't you come home more often?" Dad had said. The two of us were standing on the stoop, me jingling my keys in my hand. The outside light was on then, washing us in its glare. Mom was upstairs in her bed dying. Of course, she was still waiting for the miracle.

"It's work coming here," I'd said.

My father sat down on the step and patted the spot next to him. "Why don't we talk?"

I sat down next to him, but he didn't say anything. Not right away. I could tell something was weighing on him.

Finally, he said, "I've failed you. All of you."

I wanted to assure him that he had not, but I couldn't forget the way he always turned his back when she was breaking ours, the way he never came to our defense.

"She used to laugh a lot, you know."

"Mom?"

"Yeah, before everything."

I knew what he meant by "everything." It was no secret that he had been unfaithful to Mom since she liked to "forgive" him in front of us over and over again.

"I wanted us to be a family," he said, "but then she found God." He sniffed. "Well, Pastor Allen."

The keys were getting tighter in my hand.

"Instead of getting our marriage back on track, that sonofabitch encouraged her to make me feel like I didn't have a right to anything."

I didn't tell my father what Pastor Allen had done to me all those years earlier in his office. I didn't think it would make a difference. "I wish you two could've worked that out without destroying us," I said. "We were just kids."

"So do I, sweetheart. So do I."

I stood, kissed him lightly on the forehead and left.

Now, sitting in the darkness, I saw headlights coming down the street. Beth's car pulled in the driveway. She got out and came up the walkway. She jumped when she realized someone was sitting on the steps.

"It's just me," I said.

"Why are you out here in the dark?"

"Just thinking."

She looked around. "It is nice around here, isn't it?"

"Mmm. Beth," I said, "I'd like to talk to you."

She scooted around me, going inside and turning on the lamp. "I really don't feel like talking, Laura. It's been a long day."

"Not about the house," I said.

"Oh?"

"It's about us. I mean, when we were younger."

She eyed me with suspicion. "Who can remember that far back?"

"Well, you're right. But today, I remembered something and it came back to me like an opened floodgate."

"I knew it!" she said. "Praise Jesus!"

"What?"

"I just knew coming back to church would make you realize how much you've missed it!"

"No, Beth. I didn't miss anything. What I remembered had something to do with Pastor Allen."

Immediately, she headed toward the kitchen. I ran after her.

"I think he's responsible for a lot of what happened to us."

She turned on the stove light. "Well, he really had the spirit of God in him, didn't he?"

"He molested me, Beth."

She went to the dishwasher, opening and closing it. She folded a dishtowel, put it back on the counter, then grabbed it and folded it again. "How can you say such things about a man of God?"

"I'm worried he did the same thing to—"

The phone rang and Beth lunged for the extension on the wall near the refrigerator. After answering it, she said, "Peter Collins?"

I hesitated, then took the phone. "Peter? Please hold on one minute." Beth was pushing through the swinging door, but I put the phone down and ran after her.

"Beth, please, we need to talk."

She turned on her heel and glared at me. "You are not going to badmouth that man to me." She then raced upstairs.

I collected myself, then went back to the kitchen and picked up the phone. "Peter, how are you?" I said.

"Fine. Everything okay there?"

"Nothing out of the ordinary," I said. "I've been trying to call you all day."

"I heard," he said.

There was a moment's silence, a bit of uncertainty. "Well, I was returning your call. I just wanted to know if it was something important."

"Not really. Actually, I forget why I called. I s'pose it was to say ta for the tour."

"Oh."

"Today Claire and Graham took me to St. Patrick's. It was quite a grand service, though I must say I've been having a difficult time approaching God lately."

"I imagine," I said. "So, that was all you wanted to call about? To thank me?"

"Well, yes."

"Oh."

"I'm sorry," he said. "I did tell whomever answered the phone that was why I was calling."

"That was my sister. She left me a note that said you called. That was it." I hesitated, before saying, "Peter, there is something I'd like to discuss with you."

"Oh?"

"Nothing I can go into over the phone," I said. "It's kind of personal." There was silence. "Peter?"

"Yes, I'm here."

"How about Friday evening? There's a cute little café I had in mind."

"Friday evening?" He paused, then said, "I s'pose."

"Seven o'clock?"

"Seven is fine."

I gave him the address and said a quick goodnight. I stood in the dim lighting of the kitchen for a few minutes trying to feel hopeful. How would I be able to convince him?

I headed upstairs and tapped on Beth's bedroom door, but she didn't answer. I called from the hallway, "You okay?"

Silence.

"Beth?"

"Why wouldn't I be?"

"Beth, please. I really need to talk."

"Then do what I do and bring it to the Lord."

CHAPTER FIVE

Laura

I was huddled beneath the restaurant's green canopy; the cool, wet breeze stinging me in the face as I kept pacing. Each time a taxi pulled in front of the café, I stopped to see if it was Peter. According to my watch, it was a quarter after seven. Peter was late. Not exorbitantly late, but late enough to give me time to question what I was about to ask of him. All week long I'd been waiting for this evening, assigning seven o'clock as the hour of revelation. Maybe, though, he had no intention of showing up. I'd been stood up before and had gotten over it, but this was different.

For me, the past five days had squirmed by. I found myself trying to ignore the curious expressions at work as I hurried down the corridor to escape to my office, shut the door with a purposeful thud and hoped it would serve as a warning for anyone even thinking of interrupting my breakdown. I purposely avoided seeing Dr. Davis, too, so that she wouldn't have the opportunity to make me doubt what I was about to do. But it was Mike who finally knocked on my door then barreled in without waiting for permission to enter.

"What the hell's going on with you?" he said.

"Nothing." I stabbed the point of a pencil into some paper.

"Bullshit," he said.

I tossed the pencil and covered my face with my hands. "Just a lot of pressure on me right now."

"Your sister still not budging?"

I shook my head, grateful he assumed it was Beth and her resistance to selling the house that had me so uptight.

"Why don't you take her to court?"

I sighed. "I really don't want things to get ugly."

"Well, it's getting to you. You look wiped."

I wasn't surprised since I'd been mentally trying to figure out how to handle Peter so he wouldn't take off as if a tornado were on its way once I asked for his help. I'd even rehearsed, ad-libbing his replies with an attempted English accent. And now that it's Friday evening and he was nowhere in sight, he may have decided to totally avoid me.

Lightning flicked across the black sky, and the sky opened. A cab pulled up and at first I couldn't make out the shadow behind the rain-speckled window, but then the door opened and out climbed Peter.

I thanked the overcast heavens and then smoothed any possible wrinkles from my black dress, wondering if it was too tight, too seductive. Would one of the others left in a heap on my bed have been a wiser choice?

The taxi door slammed and Peter strode up to me, closing his umbrella. We kissed each other on the cheek and went inside to check our coats. With Peter trailing behind me, we followed the host to our table, and I began to feel like an ax-bearer leading a lamb to slaughter. Once our drink orders were taken and menus placed before us, Peter said, "Now then, do we begin with polite small talk or dive right into why you summoned me?"

"Wow," I said. "You must be in a hurry."

He shrugged. "I have a feeling I know what it is."

I raised my menu, hiding my face. "I doubt it."

"Loren put you up to this, didn't he? I imagine he's the one who told Cynthia I'm in town."

"No, he has no idea we're meeting tonight."

He studied me for a moment, as if questioning my integrity. We placed our orders and sipped our drinks. I did manage to keep the small talk going, finding one lame topic after the next keeping me from broaching the subject.

Eventually, he said, "Must be a pretty heavy topic."

"Sorry?"

"Why don't you just come out with it?"

I took a deep breath. "Peter, before I begin I need you to promise me something."

He raised his eyebrows. "Promise?"

"Please, just hear me out before you make up your mind. Or think I've lost mine."

"I'm listening." He leaned forward to confirm it.

After some hesitation, my throat tight, I said, "You know, I'm thirty years old and so what I'm about to ask is not something on a whim or something I hadn't thought hard about."

He'd finished his glass of scotch and motioned a passing waiter to bring him another. I had barely touched my wine.

"I've made a very important decision, but it's something I cannot do on my own and I need help."

His expression suddenly took on an appearance of weariness. "How much?"

"What?"

"Now that you know who Nancy Greenly really is, and the success *she's* had, you could use a drop."

"A what?"

"Er, money. Cash." The waiter placed the drink in front of Peter.

"No!" I said. "Not at all. I don't want your money."

"Then, pray tell, what is it you want?"

"I ... I want a baby."

He straightened himself. "A baby?"

I nodded.

He took a swill of his drink, then said, "I don't know what this has to do with me."

I barely paid any attention to the cod put in front of me and Peter seemed as oblivious to the steak set down in front of him.

"Laura?" he said.

"I need to do this," I said. "I need to know that nothing is as crazy as it seems."

"And a baby will help you with that?" he said.

"I know it doesn't make sense and sometimes I think it's such a selfish decision; presidents being assassinated and all the rioting going on. And we can't even figure out how to get out of Vietnam. Everything is a mess." This would be about the time Dr. Davis would tell me that I had to stop carrying the burdens of the world on my shoulders.

Peter's eyes were locked on me, his expression confused. "Yeah, it's a bloody mess, but I still don't know what this has to do with me."

As credible as possible, I said, "I'd like you to father my child."

He slammed back into the curve of his chair, running a hand through his hair. He tried to speak, but all that came out was a stutter. Then, as though the words were on tiptoe, he said, "I'm-not-sure-if-I-understand-what-you're-asking."

"Will you, you know, sleep with me?"

He gazed at me in silence for a moment but then broke into laughter. "I get it! You're doing some sort of experiment for an article. Gauging the responses and all." He finished his scotch in one fast swill. When he saw my somber expression, he said, "Laura, you can't be serious. We barely know each other."

"I know, which is perfect for me."

"Pardon?"

"I'm not looking for a relationship with anyone. Just, well, you know...."

"So, if I'm understanding correctly, you're looking for someone to impregnate you and nothing more."

"Exactly."

We were surrounded by other patrons, utensils clattering against dishes, nearby conversations flowing into discordant nonsense. Peter blinked and stroked his chin, then went to the edge of his chair as if ready to take flight. "This isn't a marriage proposal then?"

"Heavens, no!"

"Then why don't you just wait till you marry? Start a family with your husband?"

"I have no intention of getting married."

He said "oh" as if I were hiding a secret as to why.

"It's not what you think," I said. "I'll pay you. For your time."

"Is that legal?" he said. "Not that I'm considering it, but—"

"This is new territory, Peter. I don't know what's legal and what's not."

He rolled his eyes. "I just don't know how anyone could be sure that you're not lying. I mean, what if you decide to make the father responsible, financially and all? I don't think you thought this through. It's daft."

"It's not daft, and I did think it through. Once it's accomplished, you'd be done with me."

"Accomplished? That's delightful." He stopped a passing waiter and asked for another scotch, then turned back to me and said, "What if I'm a bounder who just says sure and does what you want, then become your worse nightmare?"

"Because we'd take care of the legal aspects before we try. I'll call my lawyer, you call yours. We'll sign a contract for both our protection."

"Solicitors, contracts. You are a fascinating bird, Laura." He shook his head. The waiter returned with his scotch. Peter downed it in its entirety, then said, "It's been an interesting evening, to be sure, but I've had quite enough." We hadn't touched our dinners yet, but he tossed his napkin on the table and stood.

"Please don't go!" I said. "You haven't even eaten."

He looked down at me. "I seemed to have lost my appetite."

I apologized and promised not to continue the conversation. It took my ordering him another scotch and some curious looks from those around us, but I finally got Peter to sit back down. I took a small bite of my cod and he did the same with his steak. After a moment, I said, "So, how are you liking New York?"

He chewed, swallowed, took a sip of his drink, then said, "Why me? What made you ask me?"

I paused before saying, "You appeared at the right time. And ... and, well, you're not involved right now. And you're not from around here, so there's less chance of running into you. You know, once everything falls into place."

"Once it's *accomplished*," he said, his tone sarcastic. "But what if I wanted to be involved with the child?"

"Then, we finish our dinner and say our goodbyes."

He shifted his chair closer to mine. "Why then didn't you deceive me into sleeping with you without all the bloody legalities? You get pregnant and none would be the wiser."

"I don't deal with deception. It has to be honest from the get go."

He placed his chair back with a thump and said, "You are fucking bloody mad!"

"You brought the subject up again, not me."

"I'm in shock, to be sure. Why don't you go for a younger chap, a more adventurous chap?"

"I need someone mature who won't look at this as a lark, someone who'll honor the agreement."

"I jolly well don't understand why I'm still sitting here," he said, before taking another bite of his steak.

"Good food?" I said, forcing a smile. "All I'm asking for now is that you think it over."

He didn't say anything more, but appeared to be shell-shocked. A waiter appeared and asked if there was something wrong with our dinners.

"I think we'd like the bill," Peter said.

After I paid the check, Peter stood and shook himself, as if waking from a bad dream. The conversation was in limbo, having nothing confirmed. Outside we were greeted by a furious thunderstorm, rain bouncing off the sidewalk. My car was in the garage down the block, which was where my umbrella was. Peter opened his and pulled me under it with him. "I'll walk you to your car," he said. "I'll catch a cab from there."

I wanted to argue, to pull away, but the rain was chilling and he wasn't doing anything but rushing us through the storm. Once we got to the garage, I ran in and handed the attendant my ticket. "You sure you don't need a ride?" I said.

"Absolutely." He took a step closer to me, cupping my chin in his hand. "You do seem very sincere, even if I don't understand at all your bizarre desire, Laura. I think you need to sort things out first."

"I've done all my sorting."

He hesitated, before saying, "This is certainly a strange time, isn't it?"

"What do you mean?"

"So hard to keep up, know what's what," he said. "I thought women were trying to get out of the kitchen, not want babies."

"It's about choices, Peter."

He nodded, then said, "I'll call in a few days. We'll talk some more."

Few? Three, seven, twelve? Never?

He dashed out of the garage, leaving me standing waiting for my car with nothing more than a seed of hope. Which was something I hadn't had before.

And it was good.

CHAPTER SIX

Beth

Earlier when Don galumphed over to me after Bible study and asked if I wanted to go for a cup of coffee, I said no. But the minute I pulled my bug of a car in the driveway and saw both Laura and Eric's cars out front, I wish I'd said yes. Sitting across from him would have been uncomfortable, but not nearly as uncomfortable as being trapped by two eager siblings demanding we sell the house.

I braced myself and then walked in through the front door. They weren't in the living room or the kitchen, but I heard voices coming from the backyard. I went to the backdoor and watched them through the gauzy curtains in the square of window. Eric, with his hands in his pockets, was strolling with Laura around the yard looking all chummy. The sun was beginning to set, a bright orange flame in a darkening sky. The air appeared still. Too still. It made me wonder if Laura had told Eric her suspicions about Pastor Allen. I was ready to back away when Eric noticed me and waved. There was no escape. I opened the door and walked outside.

"Hey," Eric said, "how was Bible study?"

I sighed and rolled my eyes, indicating that the same recurring problems with the same people happened once again. "Nobody is committed anymore," I said. "They say they'll come, but then don't show up."

"People are busy this time of year," Eric said. "Don understands that."

"He's nice," Laura said. "Was he there?"

"Well, he does lead it," I said.

"Do you have a minute?" Eric said.

"I have papers to grade and a test to prepare. What with Bible study and all, I have no ti—"

"We want to put the house on the market, Beth."

I plodded over to the rickety picnic table, my feet sinking into the soft ground, and slumped onto the bench creaking beneath me. "I'm not going to win, am I?"

"We'll all win, if we do it without an argument," Eric said, coming over to me. "There's a nice amount of money we could get from this place."

I looked over at Laura, who was standing by the maple tree. "You talked him into it, didn't you?" I said. She didn't respond, and I added, "This is my home."

"Technically, it's *our* home," Laura said. "But you could buy us out."

I snorted at the very idea. "I haven't had a raise in years."

"You could teach pretty much anywhere, Beth," Laura said. "And make more money at it."

"I'll get my reward in heaven."

"Beth," Eric said, "seriously, you can't do this to us."

I looked up at them. "Where will I go?"

"There's a nice complex going up a couple miles away. Wouldn't it be easier for you there than trying to take care of this place?" Eric pointed at the house with distaste. I suppose it could use a coat of paint while the shrubbery needs a good pruning.

"Why don't you at least let us get it assessed?" Laura said.

"I don't have a choice, do I?" I said.

Neither of them answered, but I already knew the answer.

Laura

"Comparatively, Miss Sumner, you won't do much better than this."

I strolled through the long, narrow, empty room. With a couch and bookcase, it would make a decent living room. Ruby, the latest agent I acquired since the cockroach fiasco, followed my every move.

I stood next to one of the double-hung windows and looked out onto East Sixty-Third Street. Not a bad location at all; one that provided a view of an actual street and not some littered alley. Basically, it was four paint-chipped walls and a hardwood floor in need of refinishing.

Red-headed Ruby must have been able to read my mind. She said, "A fresh coat of paint and some furniture, this can be something special. And the security is excellent. Paul's been the doorman here forever."

"Old, huh?" I said, taking some small pleasure in needling the desperate-for-a-sale con artist. I strolled down the hallway with Ruby fluttering behind me.

"No, not at all! He's very dependable."

I stopped at the smaller of the two bedrooms. It was tiny, but large enough for a crib and dresser. A rocking chair would fit snugly in the corner.

"Of course, you could make this your study," Ruby said. "The master bedroom is right down the hall."

I rested my head against the doorjamb. Maybe the room would be nothing more than a study. When Peter did finally contact me a few weeks earlier, my heart did double time. He immediately said he'd made no decision and couldn't think on it just then since he had to fly home. Apparently, ostensibly, his mother was ill.

I said I understood. And I did. Clearly, he was trying to avoid turning me down while turning me down. The clincher was when he'd asked for my address. I figured it would be simply to turn me down via a letter.

"See how many outlets the bedroom has?" Ruby called. "And this window seat! It really is charming."

"Ruby?" I shouted.

"Yes?"

"Shut up."

"Excuse me?"

"I'm sold. How long before I can move in?"

Ruby appeared at the end of the hall. "You'll take it?"

I nodded, realizing I was acting on faith.

Weeks later, Loren sat across from me at his desk, giving me the once-over.

"What?"

"You need some sun. You're pale."

"I don't have time to sit out in the sun."

He shook his head. "What's wrong?"

"Nothing," I said. Everything. I was discovering that active faith didn't go very far. It had been weeks since I last spoke to Peter. And waiting to hear if I was approved for my mortgage was torture. Both seemed to be taking too long for the news to be good.

"Well," Loren said, "I have an update. The book is due to release the first week of September."

I smiled a genuine smile.

"If we want this to fly, we have to get you out there plugging it for the holidays."

"I'll do whatever I have to."

"Sunny California, September."

"Oh! Telling me I was pale was a trick to get me out to the West Coast."

"Get the hell outta here. Since when do I have to trick you? You're booked for that kid's show I told you about."

"Really?"

"Yeah, then you're to meet a Mr. Klein, talk about bringing this to the big screen."

I couldn't speak for a moment. We were talking about a lot of money.

"You'll be on a book tour in between doing media. How's that going to sit with *Day's Notice?*"

"I'll quit, if I have to, but Mike might like the idea of my writing from the road. It'll be a fresh perspective."

Loren opened his drawer with some hesitation. "I have something to show you." He pulled out a manila folder and placed it inches from me. "I want you to keep an open mind."

I took the folder and opened it. At first a mass of pink was all I could make out until it finally focused into a pink goose. My pink goose. Well, not my petite feathery bird, but a life-sized costumed creation. "What's this for?"

Loren cleared his throat. "He'll be touring with you."

"*He'll* be what?"

"Sort of an insurance policy. Kids are more apt to go to a book signing if there's extra incentive. You're looking at ours."

"But you turned my goose into a gander! Talk about losing creative control."

He laughed. "That's show biz, kid."

"Anymore surprises?" I said.

"Maybe, but I'll keep you posted if it's worth it."

We both stood and he placed an arm around my shoulder as he walked me to the door. "Things moving along otherwise?"

"I hope so."

He planted a kiss on my cheek. "It'll do you good once you're back in town, looks like the commute is getting to you."

"It is." I glanced across the hall at the closed door. "Has Cynthia caught up with Peter yet?"

"Not that I'm aware."

I wasn't in the mood to go back to my office so I walked for blocks, my pace slow but my mind racing. Girls passed by in their mini-dresses and clogs, bearing a new found freedom. Eventually, I came to the conclusion that Peter was not to be the one after all, which meant I had to go through the entire spiel all over again with some other unsuspecting candidate. I wasn't quite sure I could do so.

The day rolled by and I found myself a straggler among a growing, cosmopolitan crowd with many men and few women gushing from the walls of the high-rises. They hurried past me, their stride filled with purpose.

"Could you move your ass, sister?"

I turned to find a young, emaciated woman clad in a black leotard pressing up against me. She rammed the duffle bag draped across her shoulder into my side. Can't explain why she pissed me off. I suppose Dr. Davis could have put some suggestions on the table, but I didn't bother to take the time to reason it out. I simply planted myself in front of her.

"Fuck off," she said.

"Why don't you just pirouette around me?" I said.

Before I realized what happened, the bit of woman shoved me with enough force to knock me on my ass. By the time I managed to stand back up while people swerved around me, I saw that the sprite was already across the street. I didn't bother to chase her down and decided to head back to Long Island, curl up in my bed and plan my next move.

It was past nine in the evening when I pulled into the driveway. There was a for sale sign posted on the front lawn. The sight gave me an odd feeling, as though we were selling our past to the unsuspecting. I walked into the house and heard voices coming from the kitchen. I began to head upstairs since I thought Beth might be having one of her deaconess's meetings.

"Laura, that you?"

Snagged. I put my purse down on the step and went to say a polite hello. When I pushed through the door I was surprised to see it was only Eric sitting at the table with Beth. There were coffee mugs in front of them.

"Hey," I said. "Didn't see your car out front."

"I ran over. Literally."

"Oh, what's going on?"

"Just thought I'd come over after prayer meeting," he said. "See how my sisters are doing." He studied me. "You okay?"

"Yeah." I hadn't told either of them about my putting a binder on the apartment, wanting to make certain I was approved first.

"There's more coffee," Beth said.

"No, thanks."

"Sit down and join us, anyway." Eric pushed a chair out for me.

"Where's Jenny?" I said.

"Baby-sitting for a friend. Her little one had to be rushed to the hospital."

"Oh no," I said. "Hope it's not serious."

"Don't know yet. His brother pushed him off the couch, did something to his arm. You know how kids get."

"That's right," Beth said. "They're a lot of work. It's hard enough raising them with both parents, must be impossible with one."

I didn't say anything, but started to get up.

Eric said, "Please stay. I'd like to talk to you."

Beth adjusted herself in her chair as I sat back down.

"I know I haven't said much about it till now," Eric said, "but would you mind hearing me out?"

"Go ahead," I said.

"We just care about you, Laura," he said. "I need to know, do you still plan on, well you know … having a baby?"

"Yeah."

He nodded. "Laura, aside from the fact that it's not only morally wrong, it's downright foolish."

"It might be foolish," I said, "but I don't want you telling me what you think is morally wrong."

"It's not Eric telling you," Beth said. "It's God's word."

"Laura, I think this plan of yours is draining you."

"It's the Lord speaking to you," Beth said.

Eric scowled at Beth, before saying, "I want you to be happy, but I think you're going about it the wrong way."

"That's right," Beth said, "the Lord is the only one who gives us real joy and—"

"Beth!" Eric shouted. "Will you keep quiet?" He took a paper napkin from the holder on the table and wiped his forehead. "Maybe you're starting to see the impossibility of all this."

Willing myself a renewed faith, I said, "Actually no. I've already asked someone to help me and I'm waiting for his answer."

Beth leapt from her chair. "I knew it! Didn't I tell you, Eric? Didn't I tell you that had to be what the postcard meant?"

I stopped. "Postcard?"

"I put it on your dresser. From England. I was going to throw it out, but—"

"You read my mail?" I said, vaulting from my chair. I slammed through the door and tripped over my purse as I made my frantic way upstairs. Once I reached my room, I stood outside my door, my hand trembling as I turned the knob. This, after all, was how he was going to bow out. I swung open the door, my heart pounding.

Through tear-filled eyes, across my disheveled room, I saw where my mail had been tossed. I went toward the dresser, but then, as if my slow-motion button was released, I riffled through the stack, finding ads and bills, but no postcard. I caught my breath and went through everything again, and this time the postcard fluttered to the carpet. I picked it up delicately, as though my touch might disintegrate it.

I purposely looked at the picture without really seeing it. I wanted to avoid reading his rejection. I flipped the card over. Hovering above his handwritten words was a small caption that read: Piccadilly Circus, a center for traffic and amusement. There was nothing left to do but read his message.

> *Dear Laura,*
>
> *Mother had open heart surgery, but recovering nicely. I'm still contemplating. Sometimes I wonder if you were putting me on. Were you?*
>
> *Yours truly,*
> *Peter*

I caught my breath. Where were the words, "Sorry, but no?" After reading it twice again, I clasped my hand over my mouth, muffling sounds of laughter. He hadn't actually said yes, but it wasn't the "no" I expected.

"For heaven's sake, Laura, what are you doing up there?" Beth called from the foot of the stairs.

I kissed the card, then placed it in my jewelry box. A wave of giddiness swept over me. I skipped down the stairs humming and landed with a thump on the bottom step, greeted by Eric and Beth's grim faces.

"So," Beth said, "I was right, wasn't I?"

"I got a maybe," I said, squeezing my arms. "He just might be willing to do it!"

Eric shoved his hands in his pants pockets. "Do what, Laura?"

"It!" I said.

Beth approached me head on, her eyes like beams of light. "I can't approve of this, Laura. I just can't."

"I'm not asking you to."

"Well, then," she said, running out of the house and into the front yard. Eric and I ran after her, finding her trying to pull the "For Sale" sign out of the ground.

"What are you doing?" I yelled.

"I cannot agree to sell the house. I'll be an accessory."

"An accessory?" I said. "To what?"

She kept tugging without much progress. "You know." She hissed, "You having a baby out of wedlock."

"Beth," Eric said, "we already decided to sell the house. You can't change your mind."

"Why not, Eric? You'll be an accessory, too."

"It's not any of your business!" I shouted.

A neighbor from across the street came out on to his porch. I could see the glow of his cigarette.

"We need to calm down," Eric said. "Let's get back inside."

Winded, Beth stomped by us and went up the stoop and into the house. Eric and I followed. She said, "What do you think the church'll say, Eric, when they find out we have an unwed mother living here? Not only that, but the pastor's sister!"

"Don't worry," I said. "By then I won't be living here."

"Laura, please reconsider," Eric said. "If we all just talked this through...."

"Talked what through, Eric? I'm not going to change my mind." It helped now that Peter gave me some hope. "Besides, I should be out of here in a couple of months."

"You found a place?" Eric said.

"I'm just waiting for my mortgage to get approved," I said.

Beth tried forming words, but they came out in a sputter. Then, as if she'd exhausted the fuel that kept her righteous engine running, she turned and thundered up the stairs, slamming the door shut. Eric turned to me and started to say something, but I raised a hand, stopping him.

"Please don't," I said. "I think you and Beth forget that I heard it all before."

"You don't seem to be listening, though," he said, shuffling to the living room and dropping onto the couch.

I went over and sat down next to him. "We used to be so much alike," I said. "You and me."

"Sometimes we have to put ourselves aside and live for the Lord."

"At least you learned the talk."

"Mom did what she thought was best for us."

"You think so? Sometimes I wonder if we were even a consideration."

There was a moment's silence before he said, "You just have to understand what you want to do is very serious. Putting my faith aside, I'd still think it's wrong."

"That's fine," I said. "But, Eric, how do you tell someone that they'll rot in hell simply because they are driven to do what they have to do?"

"I never said you'd rot in hell. I love you, Laura, but—"

I smashed a fist into my leg. "Don't say it if you don't mean it!"

"I do mean it!"

"Well, then you are loving someone who contradicts everything you believe."

"Not necessarily everything. And I do love *you*." He pulled me against him in a hug. "I do. And I want you to be happy."

"I will be." I paused, then said, "And I hope you and Jenny can start a family soon, too."

He loosened his hold on me. "Well, if we ever get this house sold, we're going to begin the adoption process."

"Oh, Eric! But the waiting list. It's so long."

"Well, there's this agency that's helping place orphans from Vietnam. Jenny and I would be thrilled to adopt a baby from there."

I threw my arms around his neck. "I hope we sell this place tomorrow!"

He struggled to smile. "I'd better go. Jen must be home by now." He stood. "Keep me posted about your mortgage." He hesitated, before adding, "And that English chap." He went to the door, then stopped. "Oh, and Laura."

I looked at him expectantly.

"Thanks for the money."

"Money?"

"Learn to stay out of my cabinets." He grinned and went out, closing the door behind him.

I sat for a few minutes before going into the kitchen. I washed the coffee cups, then flicked off all the lights except for the night light at the foot of the stairs. On my way up, I grabbed my purse. When I reached my bedroom, I read Peter's terse but hopeful message again.

He hadn't said no and I went to bed with that encouraging thought.

CHAPTER SEVEN

Eric

The opened Bible's worn pages do not hold my attention. If I had my choice, I'd be outside in the warm sunshine running and not in my cramped office trying to work up a sermon. Here it is a few days from Memorial Day and I want to tie the sermon in with the holiday. Usually, when the church is quiet, as it is now, with no one except me hidden away in the back office, I can whip something up in the way of a sermon in a matter of hours.

But not today.

Or even yesterday.

Actually, ever since I'd spoken with Laura the other night, I've been unable to put pen to paper, idea to completed thought. I have to admit that her passion has haunted me.

How can I tell her she's wrong when she believes with all her heart that she's right? Can that be what the Lord wants me to do? No doubt that's what the church board would expect of me. Just as they expect a relevant sermon for Memorial Day.

I looked down at the verses from Matthew, but the words were a blur lost in the memory of Beth insisting I wait for Laura that night so that I could talk sense into her. I'd tried to wangle my way out of it, but she was frantic because of that curious postcard.

"What are you doing reading other people's mail?" I'd asked her. But she was quick to tell me that the Lord led her to it. And it was up to me, "the shepherd of the flock," to talk to Laura. I reminded Beth that Laura wasn't part of our flock, but she in turn said it was up to me to change that, as well. So I agreed to stay and talk to Laura.

Now I regretted it.

Trying to convince my sister that she was wrong only started me questioning my faith. I became Jacob, but whom or what was I wrestling?

I looked up at Jenny's work of art, a brook cutting through a green pasture with a hint of blue sky behind the foliage. She'd painted it for me years ago and it means more to me than anyone can possibly know. It's the first thing I put in my office after I'd cleared out Pastor Allen's stuff. It doesn't bother me that he died in this very room; however, I am haunted by what he'd left behind. I never told a soul what I discovered in his desk, buried beneath Bible lessons and tucked in the pages of *Decision* magazine. I don't think it would be fair to bring it to light, as the man isn't here to defend himself. But who keeps such profane shots of young girls doing such obscenities? I recall how he railed against the sins of the flesh from the lectern on any number of occasions. Maybe he hoped he'd listen to his own admonitions, and maybe he would have if he hadn't been struck down with a sudden heart attack. One moment he was sorting his mail, the next, crumpled in a heap on the floor.

I threw away those magazines and decided then and there I wasn't replacing him as pastor of Seabrook Evangelical Church, but bringing freshness and life to what once felt burdensome and grim. It made my decision to preach a littler easier to accept. All these years that choice carried me along without too much question, until just the other night when Laura reminded me why I'd made the decision at all.

I never intended to pastor the church I grew up in. As a matter-of-fact, Jenny and I were all set to go to a new church in Denver where I was to serve as youth minister. Although neither of us said it, I knew Jen was thinking the same thing I was: Miles, hundreds of miles, would separate us from my mother.

But then Pastor Allen had his heart attack and I was immediately caught up in a whirlwind of events, and after a rush of meetings and votes, I found myself standing at the lectern. My letter of regret was stamped and mailed to the Denver church, and people who always called me Eric—some old enough to be my grandparents—now addressed me as Pastor Sumner.

If I had to tell you what I preached in my first sermon, I couldn't. What I do recall is after that first tirade up there on the altar in my attempt at conjuring admitted guilt, board members greeted me in the lobby with slaps on the back and hand pumping, while I wondered who was the impostor speaking such joyless words? That's when it occurred to me that I was doing my best to fit into the recently vacated slot.

However, it wasn't until I found those magazines that I gave myself permission to begin trusting my heart. And when I hung Jen's painting on the freshly painted wall, some sort of cleansing washed the room. But it wasn't until my mother's coffin was lowered in the grave that I gave myself the freedom to stake a claim on my own, very real faith.

"How's it going?"

I looked up to see Jenny standing in the doorway.

I shrugged. "Can't seem to come up with much of anything."

"Why don't you go for a run?" She came over to me, draping her arms over my shoulder. "Maybe something'll come to you then."

"That's what I've been hoping for the last two days."

She kissed my neck. "Maybe you're thinking too hard."

I glanced at my sheet of paper, filled with scratched attempts. I'd begun expanding on Beecher's quote, *Compassion cures more sins than condemnation.*

"I spoke to Mrs. Woods," she said.

"Who?"

"The caseworker at Beginnings. I told her about our selling your parents' house and buying our own."

"And?"

"She says that's really good, but we can't begin any paper work until it's a done deal."

I nodded, not surprised.

"Also, the real estate agent called."

"We have a buyer?"

She shook her head. "They can't ever find Beth at home. Whenever someone shows interest and they call, she's either not there or says she's on her way out."

"She should give them a key so they can—"

"She won't. They already asked."

"Maybe I should talk to her."

"I don't think we have a choice."

I couldn't stay in the cubbyhole of an office much longer or I'd burst. "Maybe a run would do me good," I said. I got up and hugged Jen. She fell into me, wanting more, but I couldn't give her more just then.

I escaped from the church and felt the sun rush at me. I strode down the walkway, picked up my pace and broke into a run. Sweat poured into my eyes. I knew the sermon I wanted to preach, but if I spoke of love and passion and how it fits in all the grey areas, I could easily lose my job, and no adoption agency would even consider an unemployed minister.

I began to pray, yearning for the same wisdom that guided Solomon and unquestionable faith that inspired Gideon.

Laura

It was Saturday afternoon and I was sitting at the dining room table scouring some medical books I'd checked out of the library while the Realtor, a chunky guy with glasses and beer belly, took a young couple through the house. Beth had been locked up in her bedroom ever since she returned from grocery shopping.

The couple looked at the windows in the living room while the Realtor stood off to the side.

"Studying, huh?" he said.

"Something like that."

The wife wandered into the dining room. "Why are you moving?" she said.

I looked up and said, "It's just time."

"It's a nice neighborhood?"

"Yeah."

She placed her hands on her abdomen. "Good school district?"

"Are you expecting?" I said.

She blushed and nodded. I jumped up and hugged her. "I hope to be soon, too." With help from the medical books, I was trying to understand how to determine ovulation.

She smiled. "Really? How long have you been married?"

"I'm not," I said.

Her smile vanished and she turned to look at her husband.

I said, "It's all about choices now, right?"

She gave no reply and the Realtor said, "Let me show you upstairs. There's a full bath and three bedrooms."

The phone rang and I went to the kitchen to pick it up. At first all I heard was static until a man's distant British voice broke in. "Laura?"

"Peter!" I said, too exuberantly. "Where are you?"

"Fine. Thank you.

"What?" More static.

"Dreadful connection, a storm's passing over."

"Oh, where are you? It's gorgeous here."

"Here. My parents'."

The Realtor pushed through the kitchen door. He appeared frazzled.

"Peter, hold on a minute." I looked expectantly at the Realtor.

"Your sister won't let us see her bedroom."

I held a finger up and mouthed, "Just a minute." To Peter, I said, "You're still in England?" I felt a sinking sensation of disappointment.

"They really want to see the room," the Realtor said. "For the baby."

"I can't put him on hold," I said. "He's calling from England." I put the phone back to my ear.

"... coming back—" Static. "—and I think she's sick of me."

"Who?" I said.

The Realtor waited, keeping the kitchen door ajar with his thick body.

"Mother," Peter said. "I booked a flight to New York, Tuesday evening. Ten o'clock your time."

"Great!" I said, unsure what he was leading up to.

"I wouldn't mind a lift from Kennedy. I s'pose that way we could discuss...."

"Hellooo!" I shouted into the receiver. "Peter?"

"I'm here. Bloody wicked out there. I'd best get off."

"Thank you, Peter!" I said.

"Laura, I'm not promising anything. Just can't get it off my mind."

While Peter gave me the flight number and arrival time, I did a little step dance, not caring that the Realtor was watching. After hanging up, I was jubilant.

"Your sister."

"What?" I said.

"She's not letting us in the—"

"Oh, right!" I said.

I followed him into the living room and dashed around him, practically flying up the stairs. The couple was standing in the hallway.

"We really want to see what this room looks like," the man said.

I pounded on Beth's door. She didn't answer. "Beth!" I shouted, "If you don't open the door, I am going to break it down." Still no answer. With one fast kick, the flimsy door opened. Beth was sitting on the bed, a tissue in her hand, her red eyes bugged out.

"There," I said, walking out into the hallway, "now you can see it."

I waded through a sea of people, all lugging baggage, as I made my way toward Peter. He was walking alongside a haggard-looking woman hoisting a chubby little boy on her hip. When we reached each other, he greeted me with a disconcerting kiss on the lips. I backed away.

"How was your flight?" I said, heading with him to baggage claim.

"See that little cherub over there?" He pointed at the little boy who was now sucked up in a hug by a gray-haired man. "I had the distinct pleasure of sitting next to him the entire flight. Pure bloody hell."

I laughed, but Peter stopped and turned toward me, his expression somber. "Are you sure what you want to do?"

"What do you mean?"

He pointed to the little boy.

"Absolutely!" I said. "Please don't change your mind."

"I haven't actually made it up." He grabbed a suitcase from the carousel and we headed out to the parking lot.

It was close to midnight when Peter pushed open the door to Claire and Graham's apartment he was subletting. It was already illuminated by an immense chandelier hanging from the ceiling in the cavernous living room.

"This place is huge," I said, ambling toward a window the entire length of the wall. A black marble floor mirrored the sweeping, lighted view of Manhattan.

"That's just like Claire," he said, going around the perimeter of the sunken living room to a table with a fruit basket on it. He ripped off the cellophane and offered me some grapes.

"No thanks," I said, sauntering down the carpeted steps, brushing a finger along the white leather sofa. I stopped to handle a poker in the white brick fireplace, put it back, then took the steps up to the dining room. "Just what do these people do?"

"Do? Not much of anything, really. It's old money on both sides. They don't do a hell of a lot."

"Except play host to vagabond writers?"

"Claire does love to rub elbows with the literati." He crunched into a green apple, then picked up his suitcase, motioning for me to follow.

I trailed behind, glancing to my right at the open view of an unsullied kitchen. The bathroom just down the hall was grey marble with both a toilet and bidet. Eventually, I found Peter in the bedroom, his luggage on the cream-colored carpet, his blazer tossed on the queen-sized bed. He had on an Italian T-shirt, revealing toned, defined arms.

"What?" he said.

"What do you mean, what?"

"You're giving me the most curious of looks."

I shrugged. "You must workout."

He landed on the bed. "It's all I've been doing lately." He patted the bed, inviting me to sit. I pulled out the mission-style chair from the mahogany desk and sat down.

"So...." During the drive from the airport we didn't mention the issue having drawn us together. Instead, Peter went on about his mother's operation and how his father was lost without her while she was in the hospital.

"So, indeed," Peter responded, "where do we go from here?"

I looked down, playing with my pinkie. "Well, I called my lawyer."

He raised an eyebrow. "Getting a bit ahead of yourself, no?"

"I thought you'd want to hear the legal side of things."

"He must think you were daft."

"Probably, and no matter what I have you sign, you'll still have the right to change your mind and see the child."

"S'pose it goes the other way, as well?"

I cleared my throat. "Once the child is old enough, he—or she—has a right to try and find you."

"In time for college tuition." He stood, pacing the room. "Let me guess, this solicitor said something along the lines that people change and you may end up deciding you can't handle it alone."

"I would honor the contract."

"What if that paper you work for crumbles? What if you can't sell any more books?"

"You would never know about it."

He was quiet for a moment, then said, "I say, why don't we go to your solicitor together? I'd like to hear what he has to say."

I nodded and stood. "I'll call him first thing in the morning; see what he can set up." I pushed the chair back in place. "Well, I'd better go."

"I'll walk you down," he said.

We didn't speak while walking to my car parked down the street. It was almost surreal, the arrangement we were contemplating. Other than a distant siren, it appeared New York had gone to sleep for the night; at least the New York on East Eightieth Street. I unlocked my car door.

"How about dinner, tomorrow night?" he said.

"I don't think that's a good idea," I said. "Let me make an appointment with the attorney first." I started to get into the car, but in one swift move, he reached around and pulled me to him. Before I had a chance to free myself, he fused his body with mine and kissed me.

I pushed him away. "What was that?"

"Just a goodnight kiss, Laura." He poured his hands into the pockets of his jeans and bounded to where the doorman stood.

I fell into the seat and slammed the door. I put the car in first gear and edged onto the street, then rammed the stick into second.

His kiss was warm and inviting, everything a kiss should be, but when he'd pressed his lips to mine, a tremendous weight dropped on me.

CHAPTER EIGHT

Jenny

Without telling a soul, but prematurely thanking God for answering my prayer, I believed this would be the month. God says, *blessed are those who have seen me and believed, but more blessed are those who have not seen me and believed.* And I believed, even though my history has challenged that belief. But now I'm curled up on my bed, not wanting to see anyone. And forget about praying. When I first landed here, the sun shone through the window, casting bright light into the room. Now everything was in shadows.

It was warm enough for the windows to be opened and not only did a gentle breeze flow in, but an occasional wheezy blare of the church organ from across the street. It was the first time I'd missed Wednesday evening prayer service in ages. "The cramps are too severe," I'd said to Eric earlier. It was a lie. My real problem was that I couldn't stop crying.

This was the month I was supposed to become pregnant. I believed it with all my heart.

The peal of the doorbell startled me and I lunged up. I wasn't in the mood to talk to anyone, especially one of the ladies from church. I imagined one of them took it upon herself to check up on me. I remained very still, holding my breath.

There was a second ring, followed by a persistent knock. I slipped off the bed, crept down the hall and pulled back the kitchen curtain. Laura's Thunderbird was in the driveway.

I lifted the hem of my blouse and wiped my face before going to the door. I barely opened it crack when Laura peered through and said a much too cheerful, "Hi."

I opened the door all the way and she came in.

"I *just* noticed all the cars across the street at church and realized you might be there," she said.

"I'm skipping it tonight," I said, letting my hair hang over my face in an attempt to hide my red, puffy eyes.

"You okay?" she said.

"Oh, I must be coming down with a cold," I said.

"I'm sorry," she said. "I was hoping to talk to Eric. Totally forgot about Wednesday night service."

"Well, he won't be home for awhile. Want a cup of coffee? Or something cold?" It then occurred to me that she may have some news to share. Eric told me about the postcard from some guy in England.

"You don't have to bother," she said.

"No bother," I said. "It's been so humid and they tell you to drink something hot in the winter to warm you. Then I hear on one of those talk shows that if you drink something hot in this kind of weather, it brings your body temperature down."

"Really, Jen," she said. "You don't need to…"

"Seems like they can't make up their mind." I put some mugs and the sugar on the table, then went to the refrigerator, taking out milk.

Laura sat down at the table. "Eric had asked me to keep him posted on everything, so I thought on my way back to the house tonight, I'd stop in."

Dessert. I had plenty in the freezer leftover from Easter. I took out one of the boxes Laura had brought and snapped the string. I lifted the lid, discovering brownies.

"I've been given verbal approval for the loan, so now I can actually go to contract."

I didn't realize I was holding my breath, until she didn't say anything more. I said, "So that's the news, your getting approved?"

She nodded. "Oh and I also hired a painter for the house. I'm having him start on the weekend when I'm around so Beth doesn't interfere."

"She told Eric that you went wild on Saturday and knocked her bedroom door down."

Laura shrugged. "We had interested buyers who wanted to see her room and she wouldn't let them in. The woman's pregnant and wanted to see if it would make a good nursery."

I had been doing okay, but then the tears came.

"Jen!" Laura said, jumping up, coming over and hugging me. "It's not as bad as Beth made it sound. I'm sure she exaggerated."

"No, I know. I'm sorry. Seems I'm always crying around you."

"What's wrong?"

I stepped back, wiping my eyes. "Well, just another failed month."

"Oh." She sat down. "I'm so sorry, Jen."

I pulled a chair out from the table and sat down. "I heard that you may have someone, you know, help you."

She nodded. "Who knows what will happen. I'm sure it seems very crazy to you."

Crazy? That a woman would go to such extremes? No, I understood all too well and felt guilty for it. I said, "What's he like?"

"He's nice. I think he's still in shock that I asked him."

My tears had abated. "I really don't understand how you're going to go about it. I mean, are you just going to...."

"Sort of. I mean, we're going to a lawyer first."

I must have looked foolish with my mouth dropped open because she laughed. "It's complicated," she said.

"Do you like him?" I said.

She shrugged. "Sure."

"Maybe, then, you'll end up getting married."

Laura's face darkened. "No. That's not going to happen."

I wanted to ask why, but something about her reaction stopped me. I then said, "Oh my gosh, I haven't even made the coffee yet."

"Oh, don't bother." She stood. "I really should go anyway, but please let Eric know I was by."

"It won't take a minute," I said.

"Thanks anyway," she said, "but I should do some writing tonight."

I walked her to the door and when she was gone I went back into the bedroom and curled up on the bed.

Eric

I walked into the kitchen and turned on the light to find cups and dessert on the table. I called out to Jenny, but she didn't reply. I headed down the hallway, discovering the rest of the house was dark.

"Jenny?"

I felt along the wall for the switch, flicked on the hall light and stood in the doorway barely making out Jen lying on the bed.

"Honey?" I took off my jacket and tie, tossing them on the bench at the foot of the bed. I crawled over to her, placing a hand on her stomach. "Are they unbearable?"

Instead of welcoming the soothing massage, she elbowed me away. "I don't have cramps."

"But you said...."

"I lied."

"You didn't start then?" My heart skipped at the thought that she may have been out of sorts due to pregnancy.

"Yes, I started!" She lunged up, her hair covering her face.

My hopes immediately dashed, I said, "Hon, I thought we were getting past this. I thought we were going to focus on adop—"

"*Past this?*" She scrambled off the bed. "You mean, just accept God's decision, even if I can't get *past this?*"

"It's going to happen, Jenny," I said. "I believe that. Whether you get pregnant or we adopt, we're going to have a family. God is good."

"Go to hell," she said.

Go to hell? Who was this woman?

"I don't want to hear it anymore," she shouted.

I wasn't up to a fight. Beth had drained me earlier, reminding me how wild Laura had been by knocking down her door. *She looked so demonic,*

Eric. It was like she had the strength of the devil!

My voice soft, non-combative, I said to Jenny, "Sweetheart—"

"What!" she screamed. "What, Eric, could you possibly say?"

Nothing. I could say nothing. She'd become a stranger again. A couple of months ago, after years when making love was a challenge, a contest of sorts, to see if we'd be rewarded, she'd been reawakened, happy. Sensual. And I thought she'd stopped trying, maybe thinking more about adoption. Now who was this person no longer whimpering about another infertile month but raging at the failure?

She postured in front of me, light from the hall streaming over her face, her eyes filled with fury. "Did you read today's paper?"

"What?"

"Today, did you read the paper?

I tried to recall. Sometimes one day's news bleeds into another.

"Did you see the article—pardon me—horror story, about a baby being found in a Dumpster?"

"No, I didn't see that."

"Something I want, someone else considers garbage. So I," she said, jabbing a finger into her chest, "took this as a godsend. I was even thanking Him as I dialed the social worker."

"How did you know where to call?"

"The hospital gave me the number. But when I finally got through, know what they told me?"

I didn't have to guess.

"I was the eighty-seventh caller today concerning that baby! But wait, that's not all. The baby isn't even eligible for adoption until the mother signs the papers. Throwing it in the garbage isn't good enough. Now, you tell me Mister God-Is-Good, what on earth did that baby do to deserve a start in life like that? And don't go giving me verses about the sins of the father..."

She'd stunned me into silence, but how could I let her know that I had as many questions as she had? Maybe more. I blurted, "I'm sick of people thinking of me as God's arbitrator, especially my own wife!"

The fire in her eyes died down and her tone mellowed. "It's just I don't know what to think anymore. Then Laura comes in tonight talking about wanting a baby and...."

"Laura was here?"

"Yeah, she wanted you to know that she was approved for the loan." Jen came over and sat next to me on the bed. "She's really going to extremes, you know, to get pregnant."

"Doesn't make sense," I said.

"I want to tell her she's wrong," she said, her words coming out strained, "but I'm not sure if it's because I really think it's immoral or that I just can't bear to watch her get what I can't have."

I pulled Jen into me and she didn't resist, giving in to the sobs. She rested her head on my shoulder and after some time passed, she whispered, "I'm scared, Eric. Just not sure why."

I knew why. It was those questions. She was asking them, too. All those years ago when I decided not to fall into Pastor Allen's style of grandstanding, I hadn't actually changed his message, but censured the congregation with soft-spoken words. But now, what? Will the simple message of love and tolerance get me voted out of Seabrook Evangelical Church? All that once seemed concrete was crumbling. All that was easy to preach was getting caught in reason. Years ago, I'd toyed with the idea of being an architect, but found the ways of the world were too tempting so I relented and became a minister. Now, though, designing buildings seems a whole lot less complicated than being responsible for people's souls.

Beth

When I came home from prayer meeting I found Laura asleep on the couch, the vacuum cleaner on the floor next to her. Seems she suddenly cares about the condition of this house. Here I've been taking care of it without her assistance for years, but now all of a sudden she's making sure every dust ball is sucked up, every smudge cleaned. She even put my bedroom door back on its hinges, even though it didn't make up for the fact that she'd crashed her way into my room. I walked over and put my Bible on the end table.

Laura sat up, rubbing her eyes. "Hey," she said with a yawn.

"Why you sleeping down here?"

"Can't really say," she said. "Just beat, I guess."

"Was that your car I saw earlier at the parsonage?"

She stood, stretched, then dragged the vacuum to the closet. "It was. Wanted to let Eric know what's going on. I'm going to contract."

"Oh. Well, then, you don't need the money from the house."

She turned and gave me the most incredulous look. "Eric and Jenny need the money."

"Money." I took a step toward her. "That's all anyone ever thinks about anymore. Laura, the Bible tells us that it's the root of all evil."

"Wrong, Beth," she said. "It's the *love* of money that's the root of all evil. If you're going to quote the Bible, do it right." She turned and headed upstairs.

She could be so bold at times. It was one thing to find yourself in trouble, but another to go looking for it. I ran to the end table and picked up my Bible. I knew the verse as well as I knew my own name. It was in the book of Timothy. I leafed through the pages, going to chapter six, verse ten. My finger underscored the scripture as I read it aloud: "For the love of money is the root of all evil."

I closed the Bible and let the voice chastise me.

CHAPTER NINE

Laura

A waiter bounced across the terrace toward the table where Peter and I were sitting. "Party time," he said, pouring Beaujolais into our wine glasses and leaving the bottle on the table. Then, as if carried by a gentle breeze, he floated away. I picked up my fork, ready to dip a steamed clam in melted butter, but was interrupted by Peter handing me my glass, motioning for me to raise it.

"May your dreams come true," he said.

We clinked our glasses. I put mine back down without taking a sip while Peter took a healthy swig from his.

Earlier in the week, Gloria, an old college friend, got in touch with me, wanting to go to the Jazz Festival at the seaport on Friday night. "There'll be a bunch of us," she'd said. I agreed, without mentioning that I first had to meet Peter at the attorney's office to go over the agreement. Friday finally arrived and when we were in his office, Mr. Pelton, my lawyer, had said, "And I thought we were covering new territory by trying to land on the moon." He gave his head a dubious shake, but said he would have the agreement drawn up in a matter of days. We shook hands and Peter and I walked out on to the sidewalk.

"How 'bout I take you to dinner," Peter had said, "to celebrate?"

"Oh, I can't. I'm meeting friends at South Street for a concert."

He cleared his throat and lingered. "Anyone good performing?"

I shrugged. "I really don't know. I was just told to meet my friends down there."

He wore a hopeful, little-boy expression. "I've been so bloody bored, I really would like the company," he said.

I had a couple of hours before I was to meet Gloria and the gang, so I relented, which explained why I was sitting at an outdoor café at the seaport with Peter. Once the meal was over, I figured we would go our separate ways, but Peter said, "I'm rather fond of jazz." He put his empty glass down. "Mind if I stay for the concert?"

I hesitated before saying, "You can do whatever you want."

"Well then, how do you plan to introduce me to your friends?"

I shrugged. "Why would I need to?"

He poured himself some more wine. "You're a bit of an unusual bird, Laura."

"Excuse me?"

"I just agreed to do something that I don't believe a single soul has ever done before, to help you get what you want. And now you're behaving as though I'm unpleasant."

Unpleasant? Hardly.

The waiter came with our pasta dishes, offered fresh ground pepper, then disappeared.

"I'm sorry, Peter. I *am* beyond grateful. I guess I'm just dealing with a gamut of emotions right now. And, I'm worried that we'll get to be friends."

"And that's a bad thing?"

I nodded.

After picking at some rigatoni and polishing off the bottle of wine, Peter picked up the check. I still had some time to kill so we strolled along the cobblestone path, heading toward Pier 17 where I was to meet everyone. We passed canopied carts selling all sorts of wares, then stopped to watch a street entertainer swallow a line of razor blades threaded on a string. Once he fished them back out, he shouted to the crowd surrounding him, "Still not impressed?" then pulled a playing card out of the air and sliced it with one of the blades. After a round of applause, he picked up his basket, reminding us that clapping didn't pay his bills. Peter and I darted into a nearby store called Gepettos where crates were filled with red and green wind-up toys and yo-yos. Another crate was stockpiled with small wooden Pinocchios. I picked one up and tugged on a string dangling between the legs, making the doll do a jig.

Peter laughed. "Here," he said, taking it from me, "let me get that. You can tell the baby it was a present from me."

I snatched the doll from his grasp and tossed it back into the crate, then dashed out of the store. I didn't bother to see if Peter was behind me and before I knew it, I was standing in the middle of the cobblestone path, trying to catch my breath.

"Laura?" Peter said, running up to me. "What was that back there?"

"Look," I said, "I don't think this is going to work." I started walking at a rapid rate.

"What's not going to work?" Peter said, keeping up with the pace.

"Everything. The contract, it's going to be a piece of paper, nothing more."

He gazed at me, his eyes familiar, the closeness of his body becoming comfortable. Too comfortable. I wanted more distance while desiring the intimacy.

"How did that Pelton chap term it?" Peter said. "A gentleman's agreement? Haven't I been a gentleman thus far?"

I stopped and stared at him. "You have, but I can't figure out why you are doing this. What made you agree to do it?" I was hoping Pelton would have asked those questions, but he dealt only in contracts and not therapy.

Peter hesitated, then said, "It was easier to say yes to you than no. I have no more ties to anyone, no reason not to, actually."

"But what do you care?"

A shrill whistle, pursed between a mime's hyperbolic lips, silenced us. He circled us, gave us the once over, then summoned us with his white-gloved hand.

"Let's get out of here," I mumbled, keeping my eyes down. But then a shiny silver whistle blasted again and the mime pointed directly at Peter. With a single finger, he bade him come closer. A growing crowd began to chide Peter to obey.

Out of the corner of his mouth, he said, "How do I get out of this?"

"You don't," I said. "Not without risking death."

He stepped toward the mime who broke into a triumphant grin while rallying those gathered to applaud. Once Peter reached him, the mime's shoulders shook in a devilish manner. Then, using the cutting whistle, he instructed Peter to climb several rungs on an imaginary ladder, signaling him to go higher and higher, until he reached what was supposed to be a tightrope suspended threateningly in the air. The mime directed him to walk it. The crowd screamed, warning him to be careful, as he struggled to stay on the illusory tightrope, using his extended arms for balance. Eventually the mime guided him down and made him take several bows before letting him escape.

When he reached me, he said, "S'pose I've come to like taking risks."

"Laura!"

I turned to see Gloria, draped in a granny dress, and her bell-bottomed entourage press through the crowd.

"I thought that was you," she said.

After hasty introductions all around, we went for drinks before heading to the festival. I hadn't offered any explanation to why Peter was straggling along, but once Gloria and Susan had me cornered at one end of the bar, they began grilling me.

"Now it makes sense," Gloria said.

"What does?"

"Why you and Stefanos are history."

"What do you mean?"

"Oh, Laura," Susan said, "this act is so tiresome. Your gorgeous bloke. Tell us how you met."

"We have the same literary agency. I'm sort of playing tour guide."

"Well," Gloria said, "he can't keep his eyes off you." She tossed her long brown hair over her shoulder and sipped on her rum and Coke.

"Shouldn't we get over to the festival before it gets too crowded?" I said.

The clamorous daytime merchandising had eased into a laid-back, dusky nighttime lull. Tourists had dwindled, leaving behind a conglomeration of brokers and bohemians. A double bass mesmerized the crowd as it thumped coolly in the salty breeze air. The full moon's reflection quivered on the murky East River and nearby yachts swayed to the beat. It all had a seductive, calming effect on me.

Peter leaned in, his breath warm on my neck. "Nice, isn't it?"

The bassist ended his number by giving his instrument a fast twirl and walked off stage to loud applause while an emcee walked on.

"Okay, jazz lovers," the emcee said, his voice sultry as the night air, "I'll need to say this name only once. It's all you'll ever need after you hear her sing. Gentlemen, your eyes aren't deceiving you. Please give a warm welcome for Miss Coral Breeze."

Coral Breeze? I looked over the crowd at a young woman standing motionless at the mike while hoots and whistles cut through the stillness. She began softly, timidly, but then her voice broke into a melodic rage, skipping up and down notes in a bluesy growl. The crowd cheered. I edged closer and closer toward the stage.

"She's good, isn't she?"

I looked up to see Stefanos standing next to me. There was no hello kiss, no hug—his sights were locked on Coral, who brought the crowd to its feet while she sang two more numbers. Peter found his way to where Stefanos and I were standing. Coral ended one song and over the undertones of a saxophone dedicated her next song to the love of her life, her eyes scanning the crowd and landing on Stefanos.

I turned to Peter and said, "You feel like espresso?"

We regrouped with everybody and caught a subway, jostling down to Canal Street where we found a quiet café in Little Italy. A squat balding man rushed at us as we entered.

"Please," he said, pointing to the gold watch on his thick, hairy wrist, "we're closing."

"But your sign says open," Peter said.

"Coffee and dessert only," Frank, Gloria's boyfriend, added. We all followed in a chorus of pleas. The man looked us over, muttering how we were all a bunch of hippies, then gestured to one of the many empty tables. Soon the checkered cloth was covered with pastries and various kinds of coffees. The conversation went from passionate talk about having no business being in Vietnam to hushed varied accounts of having been almost busted by the fuzz; in between there was joking and sharing of desserts. Peter brought his cannoli to my mouth. I bit into it, cream filling squirting out and running down my chin.

"Maybe you should lick it off," Susan said to Peter.

Laughing, Peter tried to dab it with his napkin, but I backed away, saying, "I got it." His expression turning from jovial to irritation, he balled up his napkin and tossed it on his plate.

Someone suggested we call it a night and soon we disbanded, leaving Peter and me standing alone on the sidewalk.

"Well, I have to get to Penn," I said. "It's late and not that many trains will be running."

"You can always stay with me," he said.

"No, I can't." I spotted a cab in the distance and hailed it. "Want to share?"

"I don't understand you," he said.

The cab pulled up and I reached for the door. "You're trying to make this more than what it should be."

"Well, I'm finding it all a bit difficult to remember when this is one lengthy bit of foreplay."

I opened the car door. "So, you wanna share?"

"No."

"You may not get another one for awhile."

"Don't worry about it," he said, his jaw tight.

I climbed in and said, "Once we hear from Mr. Pelton, then—"

Peter slammed the door and stood back. The cab roared off. I sat stunned for a moment. How could I think it wouldn't get complicated?

Why do you always need to be the one in control, Laura?

I'll have to answer that next time, my hour's up.

CHAPTER TEN

Beth

Little Kim Taylor led the congregation in a new song she'd written. She's taken guitar lessons for a couple of years now and asked Eric if it was okay she sang her song during service. The guitar outsized her small frame, but it seemed to have empowered her because she keeps belting out "Praise Jesus, he's my friend." Her long brown hair swings with the tune and if I didn't know better, I'd think it was some kind of hippie music. How could it possibly bring us closer to God any better than the inspirational hymns we've sung for years? The world is seeping into our sanctuary every which way. I think it best that we stick with what works and keep the guitar for campfires. This is something I'll have to bring up at the next deaconess meeting.

"Come on," Kim called, "join me for the refrain."

Well, I just wasn't going to, but there was Eric with a smile as wide as the ocean singing, "Let's trust in him, a good place to begin. Trust in him, a good place to begin. For Jesus is my friend."

Jenny didn't seem to be quite so enthusiastic and I took some comfort in that. But goodness, Don was almost as taken by the clamor as Eric. Even more embarrassing, he was clapping his big thick hands with the beat. And why did he take it upon himself to sit next to me the minute he came into church? Finally, Kim ended the song and sat down while some in the congregation applauded.

Eric walked to the center aisle, instead of up on the altar. Years ago, he'd made the decision to be amongst the flock during Wednesday prayer meetings, saying he thought it should be a time of unity. I don't know, though; Pastor Allen never gave up the opportunity to preach from the lectern. It kept our eyes looking upward.

"Thank you, Kim," Eric said. "That was really something. I'm sure you're parents don't regret all those lessons now."

Chuckles rippled through the church.

"Now, let's open the floor for prayer requests."

I shot my hand up high, but Eric acknowledged Doris, as if we don't know what her request will be. Sure enough, she started going on about how high her sugar has been and how the doctors can't seem to figure out why."

Once she was through, Eric said, "We'll be sure to ask the Lord to guide the doctors to an understanding."

I raised my hand again, but he recognized Charley Godwin.

"I don't have any requests, just a word of praise," Charley said. "I've found work and things are getting a bit easier on me."

Before I had a chance to put my hand in the air, Eric called on Sharon Clark, who asked us all to pray for her boy Michael, who was somewhere in Cambodia. She got choked up when she mentioned how hard it was to watch the nightly news anymore. Before she was finished talking, I shot my hand up and so did Don. Eric called on Don. I sighed in exasperation.

"I'd like to hear what Beth has to say," Don said.

Oh. I glanced at him, giving him a slight nod of thanks. Eric cleared his throat and said, "Fine."

I stood. "Well," I said, wringing my hands, "many of you already know what's been troubling me lately. I've been trying to pray about it, but my thoughts seem to get jumbled. I guess maybe the devil is getting a foothold in my home."

"Beth," Eric said, his tone warning.

"I need all your prayers for my sister. Just the other day she knocked down my bedroom door. You should have seen the evil in her eyes."

"Beth," Eric said, "please stop."

"Anyway, I was thinking if we believers could get her to listen, maybe she'd see how wrong she is."

"Thank you, Beth," Eric said.

"But, I haven't even—"

"You have our prayers," he said. "I think now we should begin."

I edged down onto my seat and soon everyone's head was bowed, taking turns praying. When Don stood, his eyes closed, his voice booming, he asked the Lord to give me peace, to help me deal with my demons. I gazed up at him. MY demons? Everyone seemed to have misunderstood me. The demons were Laura's and Laura's alone.

Once Eric closed with the final "Amen" everyone was up and about, prayer meeting having come to a close. Don leaned over. "How about joining me for some ice cream?" His brown eyes gazed at me in such a way that I could not look back.

"No, thank you," I said.

"Ah, come on," he said, his hand touching my arm.

Quickly, I stood. "I can't, Don. I have to prepare study lessons for tomorrow."

"Isn't it almost summer recess?"

"I'm starting to work on Vacation Bible School, too. And with everything going on...."

"Guess your sister has you pretty upset."

I realized by his tone that maybe I could reason with him. "Don, do you think it's such a bad idea to try and get Laura to change her mind?"

"Not at all," he said. "I don't think any woman has any business getting herself in that kind of situation."

I felt my face grow warm. "I...I was hoping we could talk to her. You know, the deacons and deaconesses."

"I don't think your brother favors that idea."

"Well, he doesn't have to know everything, does he?"

Don raised an eyebrow.

"Maybe a vanilla cone would be tasty," I said.

Laura

I walked into the house to find a collection of adolescent girls sitting around the dining room table with Beth standing at the head. She was saying, "... eager to run off to the beach, but vacation bible school is more important than getting a tan. Besides, children's souls are depending on us."

I wandered over to the table where there were placards with felt letters spelling out *Ha py In The Lord*. One of the *p*'s was out of place and I put it back.

"Laura?"

I looked at Beth and the mass of faces staring at me. "It's Father's Day," I said.

"I know."

"Shouldn't they be home with their fathers?"

"We're almost done," she said.

I headed toward the stairs, but Beth called my name and I stopped and turned.

"I miss him, too."

I couldn't say anything, my throat tight. I went upstairs to my room, closing my door. Maybe going to the cemetery hadn't been a good idea. I fell on my bed thinking back to when I got the call.

It had been a Sunday. I'd called Dad earlier in the day to tell him I didn't think I'd make it out to Long Island that day. I said I was on a deadline, but that rarely kept me from disappointing my father. Instead, I was waiting for Stefanos to return to the loft after being absent for a few days. Moments before I got the call, he walked in, looking disheveled but content. I began to question where he was when the phone rang.

"He's gone, Laura," Beth said.

"What?"

"Dad. I come home from church and find him slumped over his newspaper."

I looked up at Stefanos and knew I'd lost two men that day. Actually, if I were to be honest, I suppose I could never claim any sort of real relationship with either of them.

Now I rolled onto my side and saw the pile of papers—my work-in-progress—on my desk. But I had no desire to write. I closed my eyes. The young girls' voices from downstairs drifted up and lulled me into subconsciousness.

Remember, Eric, it's not a bat. It's a golf club.

A warm breeze blew black smoke from the barbecue, which eventually grew into a thick haze. Dad and Eric didn't appear to notice, even when the flames began to lick at the spitting chicken. Dad stood tall over a young Eric, a pimply-faced Eric. He placed his hands over Eric's on the club, showing him how to grip it.

Clouds of smoke billowed around them. "Dad," I called, "the chicken's burning." He didn't hear me, behaved as though I weren't there. My eyes stung and I couldn't see my father or brother anymore. "Daddy!" I screamed. "Make it stop!"

Then the haze was gone and Eric was nowhere to be found. Dad was standing at the grill. He turned. *Laura! What are you doing here?*

I had nothing to say, since the fire was gone.

Better get that.

That's when I recognized the sound was the phone ringing. I lunged up, gasping and sweaty.

"Laura!" Beth shouted from the bottom of the stairs. "Are you going to pick it up?"

I scrambled from the bed and ran into the hall, grabbing the extension. My hello came out muffled.

"Did I wake you?"

"Peter?" I said, having a difficult time shaking off the dream.

"Right," he said, his manner cool. "Just wanted you to know I've read over the contract."

"Yes, me too."

"I'm ready to sign it," he said.

I nodded. For a contract, it was binding enough, even though it wouldn't actually stand up in a court of law.

"You there?"

"Yes," I said, brushing away the tears.

"Well, then, you can call your solicitor and arrange for us to sign, I s'pose."

"Great," I said, shaking off the bad dream.

"Do you have a cold?" Peter said. I, too, heard the cough.

"That wasn't me," I said. "Wait."

"What's wrong?" he said.

I stopped to listen and realized that the downstairs was very quiet. The girls must have left.

"Beth, are you on the phone?"

Just then, there was a disconnecting click.

"Peter, I have to go."

"Is everything all right?"

"We had an eavesdropper," I said. "I'll call Mr. Pelton tomorrow and will let you know when he can see us."

Peter said that would be fine and I hung up, running downstairs. I found Beth in the kitchen, rinsing some cups.

"What gives you the right to listen in on my calls?" I said.

"What else can I do?" she said. "I don't know how else to deal with you."

The words were frighteningly familiar. "You don't have to *deal* with me," I said.

Beth didn't answer, not right away. Then, "Please tell me that wasn't what I think it was."

"I don't have to tell you anything," I said, and then walked out.

Finally, the contract was signed. Even though it was the middle of the afternoon, Peter and I went to celebrate with some champagne. We found a hole-in-the-wall pub, dimly lit and quiet. We chose a table in the corner and soon Peter and I were clinking our glasses, the champagne inexpensive but bubbly.

"So," I said, "if I figured out my cycle correctly, I will be ovulating on July fourth."

He appeared to be thinking, then said, "That's a fortnight away. We have to wait two weeks?"

I nodded. Thing was, my cycle was not very predictable, but once I had made the commitment to get pregnant, I began to keep a detailed journal of what my body was doing.

"But two weeks…"

"Yeah."

"And in the meantime?" he said.

"We wait. You did say you might have found your story. This'll give you time to work on it."

He pushed back from the table, the pine marred with hearts and initials of those forever in love. "True," he said. "I should get back to it, actually." He slid his empty glass away from himself to punctuate his readiness to leave.

We walked from darkness into the blinding light. I promised to call him to make the arrangements and turned my cheek to let him kiss it. Instead, he found my lips with his, but the signed contract in my purse made it so less threatening.

CHAPTER ELEVEN

Laura

I'm having a difficult time believing it is actually going to happen. Earlier in the week, I had lunch with Gloria and Susan, both who could tell that something major was going on with me. I tried to pretend that was not the case, but they finally got me to reveal what had me so distracted. Instead of sharing my enthusiasm, they stared at me as though I were losing my mind and quickly made excuses about having to get back to work. I watched as they dashed away, their heads leaned in toward each other, their voices low but incredulous. I wanted to scream out to them and ask why was it wrong that I wanted ownership to begin a pregnancy instead of having to fight for the right to terminate one. Still, their reaction didn't make me doubt myself enough to call it off.

Now, I watched as Peter's train pulled into Seabrook Station. We decided he come to the house since Beth was going to be out for the day at a church picnic. The train rolled away in a rush with Peter walking toward me on the platform. We kissed.

I pointed to the duffle bag draped across the shoulder. "It's not a sleepover," I said.

"Just a towel and bathing trunks," he said. "I may brave the ocean." Later, we were going to go down to the beach to watch the fireworks. He looked up at the sky thick with clouds. "That's if it doesn't rain."

The station was a short drive from the house. We passed Seabrook Evangelical Church and I pointed it out to Peter.

"Your brother's a parson?" he said.

"Amazing, isn't it?"

"What's amazing is how little I know about you." He drummed his fingers on his knee.

I pulled into the driveway.

"Your house is on the market?"

I nodded, pleased with how trim the hedges looked. Eric, Jenny and I had done major work on the yard in hopes of getting top dollar.

We entered the house to the smell of fresh paint and the phone ringing. "I'll get that," I said, heading toward the kitchen. "Go on up, first room on the right." I grabbed the receiver and said an impatient hello.

"Beth?"

"She's not here," I said.

"Oh, I'm having car trouble and I wanted to see if she could pick me up."

"Oh, sorry."

"Will you be going to the picnic? This is Mary."

"No, Mary. Sorry."

"Oh. Well...."

"Mary, I really need to go, but I'll give Beth your message."

"It'll be too late then."

"Sorry," I said. "I have company."

"Oh, okay. Um, well, thanks."

When I got upstairs I found Peter in my bedroom leafing through *Planning Your Pregnancy*.

I tossed my hands in the air. "They make it sound so easy."

He hummed in response and tossed it on the pile of books on the floor. I stood watching as he strolled over to my dresser and picked up a tiny framed photo. "Who's this?"

"My dad and me," I said. "Would you like some soda or water? Anything to eat?"

He shook his head and we both looked at each other. Something told me it was up to me to make the first move. I kicked off my sandals and unbuttoned my shirt, letting it fall down to my pink polished toes. After slipping out of my jeans and panties, I went over to the bed and pulled back the comforter. The only sound was the patter of raindrops on the roof. Peter came to me and I began undressing him while he brushed his lips down to my belly then back up to my mouth. Together, we fell onto the bed. I opened myself to him, wrapping my legs around his, feeling him sink inside me.

Almost instantly, shockingly, he rolled off me.

"Sorry," he whispered.

I didn't have to ask why, feeling the warmth drip down the inside of my thigh. He took a deep breath, the pillow holding his thoughts.

Eventually, I broke the silence. "What do we do now?"

"Please understand. You're the first since Cheryl died."

I wanted to cry.

"I kept telling myself it was okay, tried to imagine you were her, but then your scent, your hair...."

"Do you want me to bring you back to the train station?"

He shook his head. "God, no. I have to let go of her. Otherwise, I'll never be able to move on."

I shifted over next to him, resting my head on his shoulder. We lay quietly in each others arms without speaking. How could it have gone so wrong so fast?

Jenny

The heavens looked as if they were about to burst. All morning long the sky threatened rain, but we didn't let that discourage us from setting up the volleyball net and grills. Other beachgoers refused to give up until the sky began to grow dark, and when I looked down the long stretch of shoreline, the only people on the beach were those of us from Seabrook Evangelical Church and a dune buggy with the words *Jones Beach Safety Patrol* emblazoned on its side, heading in our direction. The moment it reached us a brawny man jumped out, trudging over to us.

"Sorry, folks, but you'll have to call it quits," he said. The same emblem on the dune buggy was also on his sleeveless shirt, which barely covered his broad, tanned chest. "There's a major storm front moving in."

"That's okay," Beth said, approaching him, wincing as the wind whipped up sand. "We have the Lord's protection."

"That may be, but I have to follow orders, which means you have to clear out. All of you."

"Thank you, sir," Eric said, clapping his hands and instructing us all to pack up. I didn't need to be told twice since a streak of lightning cut through the black.

Beth grabbed Eric's arm. "Pack it up?"

"Better hurry," the patrol officer called out, running back to his buggy. "It's coming fast."

"We answer to a higher authority," Beth shouted, her words sucked up in the wind as the dune buggy drove away.

I gathered towels and unwieldy blankets, futilely trying to shake out the sand. Eric began to help me, but Beth stopped him. "Why? Why should we listen to *him*?"

I saw the mixed look of bewilderment and concern on Eric's face.

"Beth," he said, "this is dangerous. Someone could get hurt."

She raised her hand toward the mantle of ashen sky, the black traveling across the horizon. "Fear not, sayeth the Lord, nor be dismayed, for I will be with you!"

Mary, the elderly church secretary, stumbled by chasing paper plates. She said, "I wouldn't have asked to be picked up, if I knew it'd be like this."

"Beth!" I yelled. "Come on."

She gawped at me. "But we always have a Fourth of July picnic. Always."

With the volleyball net rolled up in his grasp, Don lumbered over. "Why aren't we moving?" he shouted. Another streak of lightning ripped into the sky.

"We can use this opportunity," Beth said. "Instead of running like frightened faithless people, let's remember we're God's children! Why don't we get in a circle and—"

"Beth!" Don shouted. "The book of Hebrews tells us to obey them that rule over you, and submit yourselves...."

She stared at Don. "Why'd you say that? Th ... that man doesn't have rule over me."

"What man? I'm talking about the pastor of your church!"

Her mouth dropped and Don went back to shouting orders. Don was wise to rely on the word of God, but instead of Beth obeying she plodded closer to the churning ocean, drawing near to the crashing waves. Eric and I went to get her.

"Perhaps," she said, "it's an act of a wrathful God. Maybe it's how Moses saw Him." She looked over at us. "But Moses didn't give up." Her frustration melted into a smile and she broke away from us, heading toward the others who were making their way to their cars. "Bring it all to my house!" she shouted. "We'll set up there."

Eric stumbled after her. "Beth, you can't do that!"

"Why not?"

"There's too many of us." His wet hair blew in his eyes and he had to raise his voice over the gales. "Way too many!"

"Eric," she said, tears coming down her cheeks, "this will probably be the last time I can ever entertain in that house. Now you're not even going to let me do that?"

Rain pellets began to sting us. He gazed at her, then said, "Fine. I'll let everyone know."

She tilted her head back, rain pelting her face, her arms spread open. "Oh ye of little faith!"

Later, while Mary held the door against the strong wind, Beth and I lugged the cooler inside. It was Don who suggested we get a head start to get things ready before everybody bombarded in.

"Okay, Mary," Beth said, "you can shut the door now." She dropped her end of the cooler to push back her dripping hair. I eased my end of the cooler down. Rain blew in while Mary stood with a look of unconcern. I yelled at her to shut the door. She cupped her ear and cocked her head of white wet frizz.

"Shut the door!" Beth and I shouted in unison.

She jumped to attention and fought against gusts as she pushed the door closed. Poor Mary had a difficult enough time to hear when the wind wasn't drowning out any conversation. The three of us stood in the living room making puddles. Beth said she'd get some towels and headed toward the stairs, but then stopped on the first step.

"What's wrong?" I said.

"Someone's in the house."

"Wouldn't it be Laura?" I said. I noticed her car in the driveway when we pulled up to the house.

Beth turned and muttered, "She's not alone."

That's when I heard the creaking coming from upstairs. Bed springs. Mary just stood with her arms crossed, looking from Beth to me with a placid smile.

"Hear that?" Beth whispered to me, her eyes wide.

Mary wandered over to the bookshelf. "My, look at all these trophies."

Eager for the distraction, I said, "I haven't seen these. When did you put them out?"

"The other night," Beth said, her jaw tight. "I was hoping they'd serve as a reminder to Laura."

Mary, her arms akimbo and sights on the dining room chandelier, said, "Beth, darlin', you have an awful draft coming from somewhere."

Beth and I joined Mary as we watched the glinting crystal sway. Laura's room was directly overhead.

"I'll bet anything your heating bills could be a lot lower if you weather-stripped where that wind's getting in." She thumped into the dining room to investigate, her wet footprints leaving a trail on the rug.

Beth's voice strained, said, "People are on their way here. I can't have this going on."

I wanted to scold Laura myself, but it was not the time to do so. My voice low, I said, "Mary doesn't have a clue." We turned to see Mary's face a befuddled mass of wrinkles, trying to figure how the breeze was getting in.

"Mary!" I shouted. "Would you mind helping me get this into the kitchen?" I ran to the cooler and began to lift one end. I had to repeat myself louder before Mary dashed over. Just as we were entering the kitchen, I heard Beth's feet stomping on the stairs. I blurted hasty instructions for Mary to unload the cooler then hurried back into the living room to see Beth about halfway up the steps.

"Beth!" I said. "You can't go up there!"

"This is wrong," she said. "She can't be doing this."

Eric walked in through the front door and Beth charged back down toward him. "Do you know what she's doing up there?" she shrieked.

"Who?" he said, water dripping from him.

"Laura!"

He wiped his face on his sleeve. "Beth, calm down."

"Calm down? *Calm down?* While she's up there...fornicating?"

I noticed that the crystals had stopped swaying. Eric looked over at me for corroboration.

"She's up there," I said. I paused before adding, *"Entertaining."*

The doorbell rang and I ran to open the door while Eric led Beth into the living room. His voice was low, so I couldn't hear what he was saying, but Beth's shrill replies carried over to me.

"And you're saying we let her get away with this? She doesn't have to be accountable?"

Don walked in, lugging a cooler. Eric rushed over to help him, leaving Beth gaping at him.

It wasn't long before everyone, spilling from one room into the next, had plates of cold cuts and salads while the conversation grew louder and louder. I tried to keep an eye on Beth, hoping she wouldn't attempt to go upstairs, but she didn't need to since Laura began to pick her way down, squeezing by those who used the stairs as seating. A man followed behind her. I don't think Beth's face could have been any redder. She dashed over to her sister.

"What do you think you're doing?"

"Leaving, why?"

"You know very well why."

Everybody began to take notice of the friction in the room and the conversations began to dwindle, all attention on Laura and Beth.

"Beth," Eric said, his tone stern, "you have company."

"I know very well I have company, Eric."

"I'm not going into this with you," Laura said. "Come on, Peter."

They headed toward the door, but Beth latched on to Laura's arm. Laura turned to her and said, "Get your hands off me."

Eric ran over, prying Beth's hands off of Laura. She went out the door, with her friend following behind.

Beth stared at Eric, seething.

Laura

"You okay?" Peter said, behind the wheel of my Thunderbird. He made me give up my keys back at the house and I suppose he was right to do so. I'd argued at first, fumbling through my purse for several minutes searching for them only to find them crammed into the pocket of my jeans.

"I'll survive," I said, motioning toward the entrance to the expressway. He placed a hand on mine.

Earlier, after some time just resting in each other's arms, Peter began whispering my name, over and over again. I suppose it was to drown out the memory of Cheryl. And it worked.

I said, "Better keep both hands on the wheel." I slipped my hand out from under his.

When the house had begun to fill with voices, Peter suggested we go to his sublet. I tossed some clothes in an overnight bag, hoping to escape without a problem.

"Sad or angry?" Peter said.

"Both."

"Sometimes it's good to talk it out."

That's what Dr. Davis is for.

We eventually reached the apartment. I dropped my duffle bag on the couch and ambled over to the expansive window, the silvered view lost in a distant fog.

Peter called from the kitchen, "The fridge is rather empty." He appeared in the archway. "Like Chinese?"

His eyes were soft on me and I turned to look back at the view. "Sure," I said.

"There's a decent take-out a few squares from here, I can get us something, if you'd like."

"Sounds good," I said, looking forward to being alone to collect my thoughts. "Mind if I take a shower?"

"Be my guest," he said. 'Moo shu pork the ticket?"

I nodded.

"Be back in a bit," he said, dashing out the door.

I showered in a black marble tub, then toweled off and slipped into my red chemise. Peter hadn't returned yet, so I padded around aimlessly, my bare feet adjusting from cold tile to thick, woolly carpet. I noticed he left his duffle bag on the kitchen counter. I brought it to his room, placing it at the foot of his bed.

The last time I'd been in the sublet, he was just settling in. Now, his shirt hung on a chair and the comforter, instead of being neatly tucked, was tossed in place. A typewriter sat on a desk covered with sheets of crumpled paper; likely false starts to his work-in-progress.

I meandered over noticing tea stains on yellow-lined paper scribbled with notations. His handwriting wasn't as meticulous as it had been on the postcard he'd sent me, or even as cautious as his signature on the contract. I took a guilty look at the words: *inquisition. Contract. Keeping tabs.* (Research this.)

Any claimed guilt vanished. My stomach churned. My hands trembled. I looked at the paper rolled into the typewriter. I read enough to realize that a Linda Storm was propositioning some jerk named Paul Clark for his sperm.

I don't want it to be so medical," Linda said, her eyes moist. She tried to come off hard, unyielding, but Paul couldn't help wonder if maybe her heart, her very being, were as fragile as a desiccated butterfly.

I advanced the paper, my breath racing.

"Laura?"

I whirled around to see Peter standing in the doorway, a bag of Chinese food in his arms. The smell made me nauseous.

His expression wary, he said, "What are you doing?"

"What the hell is this?"

He looked at the paper I had ripped from the typewriter and was waving at him. "Laura, I was going to show you. I … I…."

"What?"

"I told you, I found my story."

I thought I was going to vomit. "*Your* story?"

"Quite so. There's not a bloody thing in that contract that says I can't write it."

He took a step toward me and I bolted to the other side of the room. "Get away from me."

"I didn't want you to find it this way."

"What way did you want me to find it? When it's on the bookshelves?"

"I was going to tell you. And I'm sorry if—"

"Sorry? Really?"

"Laura. I was—"

"If you're so damn sorry, then throw it out."

"Excuse me?"

"Rip it up. Burn it. Just get rid of it."

His face flushed. "Why? Just what would that accomplish? Your undying love? No, oh no, we couldn't have that now, could we? We have the fucking contract to make certain I'm out of the picture once you've sucked me dry."

"You didn't have to sign the papers, Peter. I never forced you to sign the papers."

"You're bloody rich! We both know if I hadn't we wouldn't have had today."

"What are you saying? You signed the papers just to have sex with me?"

He stared at me. "Is that what you really think?"

I didn't know what to think. I took off down the hall toward the door. He ran after me. "Laura, please. Let's talk this out."

"There's nothing to say. You've turned my life into some cheesy romance novel." I stuck my hand out. "You still have my keys."

"Why? Why do you get to leave without hearing what I have to say?"

I felt lightheaded. "Give me my keys now."

He came over, dangling them, but when I went for them, he seized my arm. "Let me go! This was all a mistake."

Still gripping me, he said, "You know, you have no idea how fucked up you are." He pressed the keys into the palm of my hand.

I reached the door, my sandals half on, my bag gaping open.

"You're really going to walk out?" he said.

"I told you, this was a mistake." I gripped the doorknob, refusing to look into his eyes.

He stepped toward me.

I pulled open the door and said, "Just leave me alone."

Beth

"Are you sure I can't do something more to clean up?" Don said. "We left you an awful mess."

Yes, it was an awful mess, but I held the door opened for Don, wishing he'd leave already. But he didn't. Instead, he stood in the doorway, shuffling his feet, trying to make conversation.

"I'm sorry your sister upset you."

"It's one of the many trials I must endure."

"Well still," he said, "there's no need for you to clean up this place on your own."

"Eric and Jenny are here. They'll help."

Just then Eric walked into the living room. "Hey, Don, sure you wouldn't care for another cup of coffee?"

Don was about to step foot back into the house, but I said, "I'm sure Don has better things to do."

"Well, I did notice your railing seems to be a bit rickety. I could come by and fix it sometime. No charge, of course."

"That'd be great, Don," Eric said.

I placed a hand on Don's back to guide him out. Beneath his cotton shirt was a back full of muscles. I pulled my hand away and shut the door without giving him a chance to say another goodbye.

Jenny came into the living room and began helping Eric collect dirty paper cups. "You two can go home," I said. "I'll get the rest."

"We're helping," Eric said.

"Well, I did bring this on myself." One glimpse told me I'd be up all night trying to remove the mud from the carpet.

Jenny was on her knees, reaching for something under the dining room table. "Why don't you let us finish in here and you start in the kitchen?"

"Well, like I said, you two can go home." I went to the kitchen and found ketchup dripping all over the counter, and whoever used my stove to fry burgers left it covered with grease. However, the worse disorder of the day was what Laura had done to the house. Desecration cannot be wiped away with soap and scalding water. And Eric's unconcerned behavior proved he was nothing but a wolf in sheep's clothing. The scales had finally fallen from my eyes.

I tossed bottle after sticky soda bottle in a large plastic bag. Jenny and Eric walked in with a stack of dirty paper plates, cups and plastic ware and shoved everything into the bag.

"The living room is done," Jenny said.

"I'll finish in here," I said. "You two go home."

"Beth," Eric said, "things are getting out of hand."

"Don't I know it!" I said. "Just wait till Laura gets back. I plan to—"

"I'm not talking about Laura. I'm talking about you."

"Me!"

"There's no need to bring the church into this."

Jenny stood near the kitchen door, twirling a strand of hair.

"As both your brother and pastor, I'm asking you to keep this between us." Without another word, he and Jenny left. I stood for a few moments, my skin getting prickly, my breathing labored.

I'm asking you to keep this between us.

I covered my ears, but I could still hear *him*. The words were familiar, the voice from the past.

What's our special bible verse? Obey them that have rule over you and submit yourselves. Hear that? Submit yourself, dear sweet, young Beth.

I wanted to finish the verse but couldn't, not with the persistent jab to gain entrance and then those horrid groans of release.

I ran from the memory, dashing into the living room. I turned on the record player, placing the needle on the album and raised the volume.

When all my labors and trials are o'er, and i am safe on that beautiful shore

I tried to sing with the hymn, struggling to keep the images out of my head.

Just to be near the dear Lord I adore, Will through the ages be glory for me.

I started pacing, noticing Mother's spider plant tipping in the curve of the rope suspended from the ceiling. I went over to it, and straightened the pot, my fingers untangling the shoots. Once again, I tried to sing, pray, anything to push away the memories, but I couldn't. Instead, I crumbled onto the floor and sobbed.

CHAPTER TWELVE

Laura

A knock sounded over the loud hum of the office air conditioner. I didn't answer, hoping whoever it was would give up and leave. No such luck. My door flung open with Mike standing in the doorway, his arms folded, his expression somber.

"What?" I said.

He strolled in and perched himself on my desk. "Security is complaining. The guys can't deal with your mood. And I'm getting pissed."

I stared at the sheet of paper in my typewriter, the words a blur.

"Now," he continued, "I want you to go down to the lobby and tell this persistent chap to leave. Ray keeps calling me. Seems he's taken a liking to this Englishman, but he says you gave him orders not to let anyone up here to see you. And Ray doesn't want to lose his job. So, please, do what you have to do to get rid of him."

I gazed up at Mike. "Peter's in the lobby now?"

"If he's the one demanding to see you, then yes, Peter's in the lobby now."

For the past month I'd been successful at avoiding him, keeping busy with my work, making plans for the book tour. Ignoring his calls. I said, "I can't."

"Why?" His brown eyes softened. "Is he threatening you?"

"Well, not really, but—"

"Then I want it done, Laura. I can't run an office with distractions like this." He stood, straightening his tie.

"Please, Mike—"

"If you value your job here, you'll do it. I have a file full of applications from writers eager to sit in that chair." He strolled out.

Soon, much too soon, the elevator whisked me down the fourteen floors, coming to a stomach-churning halt. I held my head high, kept my back straight, and strode into the cavernous lobby toward the security desk. Ray was a hulk of a man, his uniform mercilessly tight around his girth. When he saw me coming, he shifted so that Peter was now in full view.

"I'm sorry, Miss Sumner," Ray said, "but he was so darn intent on seeing you."

"You gave me little choice, Laura," Peter said. "I had to see you."

"Why?"

A smattering of people began collecting in the lobby. When the elevator departed without anyone boarding, Ray affected his orotund voice and said, "Get a move on now. This ain't no Broadway show."

"See what I'm willing to do," Peter said, pulling some papers from his back pocket and tearing them into strips.

I forced a laugh, but thought I might vomit right there in the lobby. "I still have my copy," I said. "Besides, it means nothing now."

He took a step toward me. "It means I want to see you. Forget the bloody contract."

I wanted to back away, but my legs wouldn't cooperate. "You have to leave," I said.

"Not until we talk."

"Why, need more dialogue for your potboiler?"

He sighed. "I need to explain some things."

"I'm not interested in hearing what you have to say."

"Listen," Ray said, "why don't you two go somewhere to hash this out?" I caught him giving Peter a conspiratorial wink.

"Ray," I said, "I want him out. If he doesn't leave, I'll make a formal complaint ... against you."

Ray looked apologetically at Peter. "Hey, man, sorry, but I gotta keep this job."

Peter grabbed my hand and before I could pull it away, shoved the shredded contract in it. I let the pieces flutter to the floor. He then turned, breezing through the revolving door, shouting, "When you're ready to stop being so bloody difficult, you know where to find me."

The curious assemblage stared at me in spite of Ray's prodding to move along. I strode past them and waited forever for the elevator. When it came, I got on, behaving as victor, but when the doors swept to a close, tears began to stream down my face.

With an unwieldy, overstuffed box in my arms, I felt my way down the stairs for the fifth time.

"Why do you make me repeat myself?" Beth said, from the bottom of the steps.

"Maybe," I yelled, "because your music is blasting so loud!" I stopped and added, "Did you get it fixed?"

"What?"

"The stereo."

"Yes, I bought a new needle awhile ago."

Ever since Fourth of July, Beth was relentless. The albums had been our mother's and Beth played the tinny hymns every waking hour, which could be one of the reasons why the house hadn't sold yet. Anytime an agent brought a possible buyer, she followed them around, singing along with the hymns, quoting Bible verses and making them stop at the bookshelf where she'd lined up her trophies. Eric, Jenny and I were becoming exceedingly worried about her.

Now, she said, "What are you doing?" She followed me to the red pick-up parked in the driveway. I rested the box on the opened tailgate, hopped up, pushed it back with the other cartons, and then climbed down, catching my breath. "Like I said, I went to closing. Now I'm moving."

"Whose truck is this?"

"It's a rental."

"Everything just falls into place for you, doesn't it?"

Using the sleeve of my shirt, I wiped the perspiration from my face. The August humidity clung to me, dragged me down. "Yes, Beth, after months of waiting and filling out a slew of forms, they finally decided to loan me money I have to pay back, along with loads of interest. And after writing one check out after the next at the closing, I finally get my own little bit of space. And then the moving company was so generous about giving me this truck, all I had to do was give a blood sacrifice. But you're right, everything falls into place for lucky me." I headed back into the house for another trek up to my room.

"You look ragged!" she shouted at me.

The stairs were steeper with each trip and on my way up for more belongings, I began to feel lightheaded and see stars before I stopped to sit down. Beth plopped down beside me.

"*It is well ... with my soul,*" she began singing along with the record. "It is well—" She stopped. "You okay?"

I nodded. I hadn't said anything to anyone about the disappointing end I had with Peter, but I knew they were wondering what was going on.

"Think we'll ever see each other again?" Beth said.

"Would you want to?"

"I don't approve of your lifestyle."

"Okay," I said, "but do you ever want to see me again?"

"I'm not sure, "she said, her voice cracking. "They'd be angry with me."

"Eric and Jenny?"

"No, not them."

"Who?" I said.

"What?" she said, looking at me as if I was the one not making sense.

I placed my hand on hers. "You need to talk to somebody, Beth."

"The Lord hears my prayers."

"So you've said." I got up, willed myself the strength to continue packing, and by the time I made my last trip downstairs, Beth was nowhere to be seen.

We will come rejoicing...we will come rejoicing ... we will come rejoicing.... I slammed the stereo with my hip. *B-b-bringing in the sheaves.*

I went into the kitchen to find Beth reorganizing the cabinets.

"If you need to get in touch with me," I said, "here's my address and phone number." I put the paper on the table. She didn't acknowledge me. "So ... I guess I'll go over and say goodbye to Eric and Jenny."

"They're not home," Beth said, her voice low. "Decided to go away this week. The shepherd abandons his flock to *honeymoon* in Niagara Falls."

There was nothing else to say. On my way out I noticed the dozens of shoots suspended from the spider plant. A blaring organ was coming from the stereo. I went over and lifted a tendril. If I snapped it off and tried to root it, I wondered if it would survive. Flourish even. Just then the organ screeched to a silence, the needle scratching across the record. I turned, surprised to see Beth standing at the stereo, her body trembling.

"Beth?"

She spun around, wiping her face. "I thought you left!"

I let the tendril fall into place and went over to her. "I know something happened, Beth. Pastor Al—"

She bellowed, "Obey them that have rule over you and submit yourselves!"

I nodded and walked out.

The first piece of mail that was forwarded to my new address was Stefanos' wedding invitation. I hadn't planned on attending, but then his Aunt Angie called me at work. She insisted I go. "He needs to be reminded what he's giving up!" she said over the phone. I envisioned her small wiry body twitching as she spoke.

"According to your nephew," I said, "we were never officially a couple."

"Please, Laura. Come for an old woman. I don't know how long I have left."

I couldn't help but smile, since she used that same guilt-inducing statement from when I first met her. Before I knew it, the dreaded day came and I watched my former live-in pledge fidelity to his raven-haired goddess in some cheesy catering hall in Queens. Aunt Angie had me sit at her table at the reception.

"Taste," she said, bringing some mishmash to my lips.

"What is it?"

"Always questions with you! Kakavia. Now taste."

I took a bite and the mishmash got caught in my throat before I forced it down. Then the rattle of a tambourine began. Soon violins and drums joined in and the dance floor filled. I remained seated next to Aunt Angie at the table until she yelled over to Stefanos' gangly cousin. "Dimitri, come!"

"What, Aunt Angie?" he said, running over to her, his arms and legs seemingly too long for his adolescent body.

"Dance with Laura," she said.

"Oh, no. No, really," I said, just as Dimitri, a boy in a man's body, dragged me onto the dance floor.

"We must obey my aunt," he shouted, whirling me to the center of a circle.

Stefanos stood on the perimeter, clapping and shouting. Hoots and howls cheered us on, me a rag doll under Dimitri's giddy power. My demands didn't discourage him from spinning me. My glare did not stop him from twirling me; whirling, twirling, faces whirring by, my stomach roiling. I wanted to warn him, but the puppeteer was too lost in his wild gyrations to notice, and in a few mortifying seconds I reduced the room to a sudden, shocked hush: Limp green chunks stewed in retsina spewed from my heaving insides and onto Dimitri's shiny black shoes. The deactivated fool's mouth was agape as he watched the spew pool on and around his oversized feet.

"Come, come," Aunt Angie said, grabbing me by the hand and dragging me off to the bathroom.

I tossed some water on my face. "Well, I'm sure Stefanos isn't having any regrets now, Aunt Angie," I said.

She waved her hands. "Eck, he will soon enough. Mind my words."

I rolled out some paper towels, dried my face and gave Aunt Angie a hug. "I'm going to go now."

I kissed her on the cheek, then walked outside and hailed a cab to drive me back into the city, back to my new home.

A couple of weeks after that embarrassing scene I found myself far away in a television studio in Los Angeles.

"Okay, Miss Sumner," a stagehand said, "we'll be bringing the kids on any second. Why don't you get settled right over there."

I followed the direction his stubby finger pointed to and noticed a chair planted in the middle of the set, which resembled the play-room of any well-to-do child, but was actually the set for *Kid Talk*.

I said, "Does that chair need to be there?"

"Where else you gonna sit?" the stagehand said.

I shrugged. "On the floor, with the kids."

He scurried over to the director, grumbling and pointing from the chair to me.

I called over, "If it's too big a deal, then don't worry about it." I didn't want to acquire a reputation for being difficult. I'd been in LA for a few days, working on the film adaptation for the book and argued against some of the inane adventures proposed for the feathered creature. Loren had warned me that news travels fast and no one was willing to work with a difficult author. Eventually, compromises were made.

"Wonderful!" the director called over. "I love it. Don't know why I didn't think of it myself." He clapped his hands in double time. "Gary, we need to change the lighting."

The chair was whisked off the set and I was told to come on, along with about a dozen boys and girls. I edged down to the floor, my skirt floating around me. The children, some with missing teeth, others groomed to nauseating perfection, formed a half circle in front of me.

I started to ask what their names were, when a voice in the shadows shouted, "Three, two, one. And we're on."

I gazed at the wide-eyed faces, all blinded by the bright lights. I said, "So, who wants to hear a story?"

One little boy discovered himself on the monitor and pointed at it. Quickly, I flamboyantly cracked open the book and said, "Want to hear the story of *The Pink Goose*?"

I had their attention, the little boy included. "This is a rhyming story about...," I paused for effect, "... *The Pink Goose*." Up from the first page sprang a bright pink goose with a real pink tail feather. The children gasped and I began to read.

"The day began splendid on the busy farm
That is until Goose appeared, causing great alarm
She waddled into the barnyard with nowhere to hide
"Your feathers are pink!" the animals all cried
True, somehow she awoke to be a peculiar pink shade
But white had been perfect, white had made the grade

Tony the pony gave her mane a disapproving shake
Mama pig gathered her piglets for their precious sake
With a swish of his tail and a loud snort
Jeremiah the bull demanded Goose appear in court
"You're a bird, but not a flamingo!" insisted the judge
A goose should be white, from that he would not budge

Whinnying and mooing, they all agreed
The decision had been determinedly decreed
Suddenly, the pink goose flapped her wings madly
After all, she hadn't behaved all that badly
It wasn't her fault she was the startling color
She'd be happy with something much, much duller

She flapped and objected; the animals stared in disbelief
Goose ran from here to there shouting, "Good grief, good grief!"
But fluttering her feathers in all the commotion
Had been the perfect, the absolute, magic potion
Her once-pink fluff was now turning white
Goose had suddenly become…well, an ordinary sight

Yes, the plumage was white, save for one on the ground
Goose stared at it without making a sound
Yes, she was ordinary and it caused her to weep
While the chicks and ducklings didn't make a peep
Now it was too late to be grateful for what she'd had
She wandered away, for she was very sad

Their hasty judgment the animals began to regret
Silently wishing for a pink feather to pet
Tony the pony realized it had been quite rare
Mama pig didn't know why she'd even care
Jeremiah the bull thought the day no longer sunny
While the bumblebees hadn't any desire to make sweet honey

But then, amazingly, the pink hue returned
A lesson without a doubt was about to be learned
It was nice to be different, as a matter-of-fact, the best
For now it was clear Goose couldn't be like the rest
There was celebration of the return of the soft PINK down
Goose strutting as if wearing a glorious crown

So, let me advise you, and say it loud
It's great being an original in a very common crowd
Just as Goose first regretted being pink
She'll warn you profusely to stop and think
Don't go seeking to find what's not there
For you are you, wonderful and rare."

It was a magical book, one with clever illustrations designed to pop up with each turning page and it seemed to have entertained the children with a response of "oohs" and "ahhs." Then a life-sized pink goose waddled on-stage and children jumped up, running over to touch the neon-pink plumes. They surrounded the goose, chattering.

"And, we're out," someone yelled. "Good segment, Miss Sumner."

As quickly as I stood up, I went back down, finding myself plummeting into a galaxy of tiny stars. I'm not sure how much time had gone by when I heard my name being called.

"Miss Sumner? Miss Sumner, are you all right?"

I opened my eyes and saw a ceiling of faces bent over my sprawled body.

"You passed out," someone said.

"Where are the kids?" I shifted up onto my elbow.

"The goose herded them into the back."

"Good," I muttered, taking a cup of water someone handed me. I took a sip, feeling foolish with everyone amassed around me. "Those lights are killers."

"Yeah, especially if you're not used to them," the director said. "Would you like someone to drive you to your hotel?"

"That'd be nice." Room service and a soak in a hot tub would be extra nice. I'd been going non-stop promoting the book. Still, I wasn't complaining. I appreciated the distractions. They kept me from hoping too much.

"Something to be said for promotion," I said to the bookseller standing next to me while one child after the next approached the table. While the costumed pink goose entertained the children on line, I scribbled my signature over and over again. I couldn't help but think how ruinous it could have been had I not shown up, but by the way I'd felt the night before that had been a possibility.

I'd ordered room service as intended, but after two small bites of chicken, my body rejected it in a most violent way. Grasping the sides of the toilet bowl, I suffered exhausting paroxysms and a bloody nose before crumpling onto the cold tile floor. It took all my strength to crawl over to the bed and flop down on it. A book tour was not the time to become ill and it should have upset me. But it didn't. Curled under my covers, I fell asleep with a smile on what had to be a serene face.

By morning, I felt much better. Wasn't something in reverse? The idea made me wonder if perhaps I was jumping to conclusions. Still, there had been little time to sort it all out, so I got dressed and headed to the book signing, which was now going quite well.

"Well, Miss Sumner, how are we doing today?"

I did a double take, then broke into a smile, jumping up. "Loren!" At a dizzying speed, I dropped back down.

"Whoa, whoa, take it easy," he said, reaching out to steady me.

"It's so good to see you," I said, getting my balance back, and hugging him. "This has been such a lonely tour."

"What's wrong, you and the goose squabble?" He made himself laugh.

"I should be jealous. He's ... she's getting more attention than me."

"Yeah, but she's selling books for you." He stopped, looking me over. "So, you have a rough night last night?"

"It shows?"

"To be honest, yeah. And what's this I hear about your fainting on the set yesterday?"

"That's the reason for your surprise drop in?" I said.

He shrugged. "I had business here anyway."

I summoned a fidgeting child over and took the book.

"How 'bout dinner?" Loren said.

"That'd be great," I said.

"Good. And maybe I'll convince you to see a doctor. You look like hell." He glimpsed the pig-tailed little girl standing nearby and the scowl of her disapproving mother.

"I mean," he said, "you don't look so *well*."

"Maybe I have a good reason," I said, blowing him a kiss.

It had been easier rationalizing the embarrassing scene at Stefanos' wedding by blaming the combination of various foods sloshed around by a dancing fool than from my unprovoked vomiting the night before. Excuses were becoming more difficult to come by.

Loren was right and it was time to see a doctor.

CHAPTER THIRTEEN

Beth

"Sorry to disturb you, Dea … Don, but I really need to discuss something with you." I stood outside Don's front door, his dog barking in wild protest. "Is it a bad time?"

"No, no," Don said, appearing flustered. He used one hand to hold back the golden retriever, the other to stop the door from closing on me.

"Maybe I should have called first," I said.

"Don't be silly. You're a ray of sunshine."

I felt myself blush. No one ever called me that before. I walked into the kitchen, standing as far back from the yipping mongrel as possible.

"Down, Clyde!" Don said, his tone harsh. Surprisingly, the dog obeyed.

"He doesn't see many people," Don said. He went to the table, shoved a pile of newspapers to the side, and pulled out a chair, also filled with papers and magazines. He put them on the counter, then gestured for me to sit.

"Coffee?" he said.

"That's not necessary."

"No problem," he said, going to the stove and lighting a jet under a greasy teakettle. "Helen used to always have a pot of coffee on for any unexpected company." He surveyed the room, as if for the first time. "She'd be mad as anything if she saw the way I let this place go."

I sat quietly, letting him go on.

"Still can't believe she's gone," he said, going to the cabinet and taking out a jar of instant coffee.

"She was a good woman," I said. "A godly woman."

"She sure was at that."

"It would upset her to see what's happening at the church," I said.

Don took a mug out of the dish rack and another from the cabinet. "What do you mean?"

"Well, all the outside influences that are starting to compromise us."

He scooped some coffee into the mugs. "I'm not sure I know what you mean."

I brushed some crumbs from the vinyl tablecloth into the palm of my hand.

"Here," Don said, reaching over and cupping his hands. I poured the crumbs into them. "Helen was the housekeeper," he said, dumping the crumbs in the garbage.

"We all miss her."

"Oh, it's not so bad anymore. Me and Clyde make do." The dog lifted his head at his name, but stayed in place. "But I do miss the presence of a good woman."

I avoided making eye contact with him and said, "Don, I can't even get Eric to listen to me."

The teakettle came to a low whistle. He filled the cups with the hot water and brought them to the table.

"I don't have any dessert," he said, going to the refrigerator and taking out some milk.

"That's not necessary."

He put the milk on the table and pushed a sugar bowl toward me. "I could run to the store—"

"Don! I didn't come here to be entertained, for goodness sake."

"Oh, sorry," he said, pulling out a chair and sitting down.

"Like I was saying, Eric doesn't want to listen to me. I mean, I took in Laura after Dad died. She left her boyfriend and needed a place to live. And the Christian thing to do was to take her in. I knew about her sinful ways, but I was hoping I could help her."

"Huh," Don said.

"But then you saw how she embarrassed me that day at the house with that man and then she up and leaves me with all the bills and headache of having to show the house."

"I'm sure Eric is concerned, Beth," Don said. "He's also a very compassionate man."

"Mother would call him soft."

"Yes, she would have," Don said. "She was a woman with very little tolerance."

"Tolerance gives the devil a foothold. Which is why I'd like for us to call a meeting."

"A meeting?" He took a sip of his coffee.

"Eric's changed. Anybody can see that. Don, he didn't even have altar call at Easter Service!"

"So, what would be the purpose for this meeting?"

"To put Eric on notice."

"Notice? Why?"

"Don't tell me you don't see how he's changed. His sermons are all wishy washy."

"Beth, I know that Eric is very concerned about what Laura wants to do, but she's a grown woman. She can make her own decisions."

"She'll go to hell for it."

"Sounds like your mother talking."

"She was blessed with wisdom."

Clyde ambled in and Don scratched him behind his ear. "I have to tell you, Beth, I think Eric is doing just fine. A little compassion in today's world seems kind of refreshing."

"But it's our responsibility to show the world—"

He took my hand. "That's right, Beth, show, but not force. Why don't we bring your concerns before the Lord right now?" Without waiting, he closed his eyes and began to pray.

I tried to listen, but a jumble of voices in my head made nothing but noise. I couldn't close my eyes, watching his hand caress mine.

"We ask for your guidance in Beth's life, Lord...." Don's head was bowed while he caressed Clyde with his other hand. The mutt panted, his wet tongue lolling. "Please give her an understanding...."

Don's thumb kept caressing my hand while he went on talking, his voice pleading God to give me an understanding that passes all understanding. I pulled my hand away and jumped up from my chair, splashing the coffee from our cups. Clyde stood on all fours and growled.

"Beth," Don said.

"All everyone does anymore is pray." I grabbed my purse and was out the door, but just as I reached the car, a hand grabbed my arm. I screamed, telling him to let go. I jumped into my car and backed out. When I dared to glance, Don, with a look of bewilderment, was standing in the driveway.

CHAPTER FOURTEEN

Laura

When I'd left New York to go on tour the season was summer, the leaves green. Now, it's autumn and I am looking forward to seeing the brilliant reds and oranges. I pressed my face against the small window as we taxied down the runway, picked up speed, then took the committed leap. I rested my hand on my fluttering belly and gazed down on Atlanta until clouds blocked it from sight. I whispered a sweet goodbye to the place where I'd discovered what I'd hoped was true all along.

It had been a yellow-page search that led me to a local doctor. The waiting room was paneled with some dark, cheap, compressed wood; the magazines were tattered and musty-smelling. And there was dust on the end tables. I was about to walk out when I was summoned into the doctor's examining room.

"So, what makes you think you're pregnant, Mrs. Sumner?" the doctor, whose hair looked like unruly steel wool, said.

"Miss," I said. "I'm not married."

He looked at me over the rim of his glasses.

"My period has never been all that regular, but I—"

"Hmm," he said, his jowls quivering. "So you got yourself caught."

"Oh, no," I said. "I—"

"Git your clothes off and Dottie'll do the preliminaries." He headed out the door mumbling about irresponsible women.

As soon as I slipped out of my clothes, Dottie was there holding out a robe. "Get on the scale," she said.

"Is that really necessary?"

"For a bit of a thing like you?" Dottie chuckled. "You don't have a thing to worry 'bout, darlin'." She slid the weight to the right, then back to the left again. "You're a long way from home to be seeing a doctor."

"I know, but I've been on tour and—"

"You a singer?" Dottie patted the examining table.

"Not even in my wildest dreams," I said, the sanitized paper crinkling loudly. "I'm a writer."

"Oh my, we never had no celebrity in here before. I just love to read myself. Every morning with my coffee, I have some romance in front of me." She cuffed my arm and began pumping.

"Ever read any Nancy Greenly novels?" I said.

"Oh, yes, but she hasn't come out with anything in quite awhile."

I didn't say anything more, not sure why I even mentioned Peter's creation.

The doctor walked in. "Why don't you give it a rest, Dottie." He looked at the chart, then instructed me to lie down and began kneading my abdomen.

"When was your last menstration?"

"June."

"Relax," he said, tunneling one hand inward and manipulating my outer stomach with his other. A moment later he snapped off his gloves. "I'll need some blood."

"Blood?"

"It'll make things more clear." He left the room, saying he'd see me in his office once I was dressed.

"He always wants blood samples," Dottie said, jabbing my finger and filling a skinny glass tube with the dark liquid. "So your boyfriend know?"

"I don't have a boyfriend."

She gave me a disapproving look as she handed me a cotton ball. "Once you're dressed, the doctor'll see you in his office."

I took my time dressing, my hands shaking, wondering if I were imagining the exhaustion and late night nausea; the twinges and aches. The cotton ball soaked through so I helped myself to another one. Finally, I braced myself and crossed the hall, hesitating outside the doctor's door. It was open and he was sitting at his desk, bent over some notes.

"Well, what you waitin' on?" he said, without looking up. "Come, have a seat."

I barely sat down when he said, "You're close to being twelve weeks along."

I gasped, falling back in the chair. It had been twelve long weeks of determined distractions.

"Dottie!" he called. When she appeared in the doorway, he said, "Git her more cotton for that finger."

I looked down to see that the second cotton ball was soaked with blood.

The doctor handed me a slip of paper with a phone number on it.

"What's this?"

"You call that number. They'll help you."

"Help me?"

"I wouldn't wait too much longer. Gets dangerous."

"Oh, no!" I said, tossing the paper back at him. "I want this baby. I planned it."

"But you said you weren't married."

"I'm not."

He regarded me for a moment, then said, "You find yourself tired, feeling faint?"

I nodded, taking the fresh cotton ball from Dottie, who disappeared almost as quickly as she'd appeared.

"You're anemic. Iron pills should take care of that."

Now I was heading home—my new home, even though it was barely furnished. But still, it was home and in just a few months it would be all the more so.

"You're back! Eric and I have been trying to reach you all day."

"Jenny?" I said, sitting up in bed, rubbing the grogginess from my eyes.

"Did I wake you?" she said. "We just got back from evening service and thought we'd try you one more time. Your postcard said you'd be home this weekend and we couldn't wait to hear how you're doing."

I fumbled with the clock on my nightstand. Nine o'clock. "Got in a little while ago," I said. I could just make out the shadows of my luggage piled in the corner. I'd been too exhausted to unpack when I got in.

"... can't wait to hear about the tour. I see your book all over."

I tried to stay focused on what she was saying, but more than anything wanted to fall back onto my pillow and sleep.

"We're wondering when we can visit. We haven't seen your place yet. And, oh, we have someone interested in the house. They put a binder on it."

"That's good news," I said.

Is this Saturday good for you?"

"This Saturday?"

"I mean, unless you're busy. Eric and I have a little housewarming gift for you and wanted to see--"

I had no idea if Saturday was good or not, but said, "Sure."

"Around two o'clock would be good for us. Eric has a meeting in the morning, but that's about it for the day."

"Okay," I said, thinking of my empty kitchen cabinets, the tiny table made for two. "Maybe we could go out for dinner," I said.

"That would be fun," she said. "We have so much to talk to you about."

That's when it occurred to me that her jubilation may be from her own good news. Wouldn't that be something, the two of us pregnant at the same time! "Jenny," I said, "I have some news."

There was the slight hesitation instead of the expected, *I have news, too!* She said, "What?"

"Well, I don't want to upset you."

Silence.

"Jenny?"

"I'm here."

"I'm—"

"Pregnant," she said.

"You, too?" I said.

"No," she said. "I was just guessing what you were going to say."

"Oh, Jenny. I'm sorry."

More silence.

"Jenny, you there?"

"That's ... that's.... Wow." Then, hastily, she said, "Eric wants to talk to you."

There were muffled voices, whispers, a prodding for Eric to get on the phone. Finally, he said, "Hey, Sis."

"Is Jenny okay?"

He paused before saying, "She'll be fine. I wish it were different, wish I could congratulate you."

"Eric, I'm sorry. I don't like that it's not happening for you, too, but can't you at least be happy for me a little bit?"

"Listen," he said, "I'm not trying to meddle, but you'd better let me be the one to break it to Beth."

"*Break it* to Beth?"

"She's been a little, well...." He hesitated. "... wild lately, on a spiritual warpath."

"Worse than usual?"

"You could say that," he said.

I groaned. "Is it because someone may actually buy the house?"

"That doesn't help, but it's more like she's on a mission to rid the world of evil."

"And I suppose I'm the prime target."

"Pretty much. So, is it okay if I tell her?"

"Sure," I said. "But Eric, once the house gets sold you and Jenny can begin the adoption process, right?"

"Funny how everything else gets diminished by that single obsession," he said.

"Was that meant for me?"

"Not intentionally."

"Will you still be coming on Saturday?"

"I will. Can't speak for Jenny."

After we said our goodbyes, I put my head on the pillow and immediately fell back to sleep.

The next day I went to *Day's Notice* office. I said a hasty hello to Ray as I walked by him toward the elevator. I hadn't decided if I would tell Mike my news right away or wait, but when he walked into my office as I was sorting through my mail, he said, "Rough trip?"

"Not really," I said, tossing some junk mail in the garbage. "The publisher is very happy."

"What about you?" he said.

I looked up. "I'm thrilled." That's when I spilled my news. I didn't see any reason not to.

He sat down on the corner of my desk. "You keeping it?"

"Of course! I wanted it."

He raised an eyebrow. "So, is this your way of giving your notice?" he said.

"Not at all. I just wanted you to know."

"All you women are the same," he said, "thinking you can have it both ways. Pretty soon, you'll miss one deadline after the next and fall into that confounding world of motherhood."

"If I leave this job, it won't be because of the baby," I said.

He straightened his back, turned on his heel and walked out. I picked up the phone and dialed Dawn. After I asked her about sweet Aisia, I told her my news.

"And you planned this, girl?" Dawn said, her tone stunned.

"I did."

She lowered her voice in a whisper. "Who's the father?"

"No one you know," I said. "Dawn, just be happy for me. I need *someone* to be happy for me."

She sighed. "I hope you know what you're in for. When are you due?"

"I don't know. That's why I kind of need the name of your gynecologist."

"You don't have a gynecologist?"

I cleared my throat. The kind of doctors I always sought were those who dealt with my psyche. "No," I said.

Dawn said, "Let me call my Ob/gyn and see what I can do and I'll get right back to you."

"Thanks," I said. I hung up and went back to sorting mail. A short time later, Dawn called back. "He can see you tomorrow."

"Tomorrow? Wow, that's fast," I said.

"Girl, you should've gone to him before this."

The following day when I walked into my office I discovered a long, narrow box taking up most of my desk.

"Hey, Laura," Mike said, appearing at the door. "I need a piece about Twiggy."

I looked up and smiled. "Thanks."

"For what? You a Twiggy fan?"

"No, these," I said, touching the box of flowers.

"Those aren't from me or anybody here far as I know. Anyway, I need the story by noon tomorrow. She's in town and—"

Without bothering to take off my long, wool coat, I slid the ribbon down and tugged off the cardboard lid. Twelve buttery white roses rested in a bed of baby's breath.

"Got that?" Mike said.

"Sure," I said, not at all certain what he'd said. He walked out and I opened the gift card.

Dear Laura,
Please give us a chance. — Peter

I threw the card into the box, smashed the lid on and shoved the whole thing into the wastebasket, even though it didn't fit. I fell into my chair, covering my hand over my mouth in an attempt to control my breathing. I was sure he'd given up by now. The thought had been confirmed when I had no messages from him once I'd returned from my tour. Just then, Ray's round face with a twinkle in his eye came to mind.

I riffled through the Rolodex, then picked up the phone and dialed.

"Allo?" said a female voice.

"Peter ... Peter Collins, please."

"Oh, sorry. Peter's moved out."

"Oh," I said. "Back to London?"

"No. Graham and I are so delighted he took a flat here in the city. Now, if you give me your name and number, I'll call him with your information."

My nose started to drip and I grabbed a tissue from the box on my desk. "Peter's staying here? In the city?"

"Amusing, eh what? With all his grumbling 'bout the hustle and bustle, being too close to his agent."

I was startled to see blood on the tissue.

"He did ask, though, that I not give out his number, but I can give him a message."

Dabbing at my nose, I said, "Tell him Laura called and said to leave her alone. No more flowers, no phone calls. Just leave her alone." I then dropped the receiver down.

"Hellooo, Laura? Laura, you there?"

I looked up to see Dawn with Aisia in her arms.

"Thought I'd come over and give this to you." She handed me a box, gift wrapped with a bright yellow bow. "I think you're nuts to do this all by yourself, but it's---Laura, good grief!" She handed me a wad of tissues.

Peter took up residency in manhattan?

"Good thing you're seeing Dr. Kim today."

He said he hated New York.

"Hey, why did you throw these out? They're beautiful!"

"It would've been smarter to come to me *before* getting pregnant," Dr. Kim said. "And once you suspected as much, why did you wait?"

"Well," I said, tucking my blouse into my skirt, relieved that the probing and prodding was over, "I've been out of town."

The doctor had his back to me, writing on a chart. "How well do you know the father, his medical history?"

I shrugged and he turned to look at me. "Your due date is somewhere around the middle of April. I want to see you again in a month, unless there's a problem."

"Like what?"

"A number of things. Staining. If the lab report comes back with something suspicious."

"I'm sure I'll feel better once I start taking the iron pills," I said.

"Well, rest when you can and even when you cannot."

I gathered my belongings, slipping a pile of pamphlets Dr. Kim gave me into my purse. April. Flowers would be blooming, the air warm; a perfect time to bring a baby into the world.

"Too bad the tour was so grueling," Loren said, sitting across from me at his desk.

I willed myself to glow. "The tour was fine, sold a lot of books."

He straightened in his chair and broke into a smile. "Well, you're right about that. The book is moving right up the lists, Laura. We plan to keep it that way. You know how to skate?"

"Skate, why?"

"You and your goose have been invited to appear at Rockefeller Center for Thanksgiving weekend. Oh, and get this, the Pink Goose is going to be in the parade."

"*The* parade?" I said.

He swiveled in his chair and shouted, "I love your goose, Laura!"

I laughed, only to realize that my nose was bleeding again, blood cascading onto my coat. I searched my pockets for a tissue.

"Holy Jesus!" Loren handed me a handkerchief he'd pulled from his pocket. "I don't like this, Laura."

"Relax," I said, stanching the flow.

"I'm telling you, I want you to see a doctor."

"I just did," I said. "And there is a reason for all of this."

He leaned in, his face somber.

"I'm going to have a baby."

He scowled, fell back into his chair. "You're what?"

"I'm going to have a baby."

"Oh, shit. Laura...."

"What, Loren? It's something I wanted."

He studied me for a moment. "Wanted?"

The bleeding stopped and I crumpled the handkerchief in my hand. "Yeah, I planned it."

"I didn't know you were dating anyone."

"I'm not."

He was tongue-tied, but then said, "Do I want to know the details?"

"Even if you did, I wouldn't tell you."

"And that's the reason for the bloody nose, how pale you look?"

I nodded. "Well, aren't you going to congratulate me?"

He scowled. "You can handle this?"

"Women have been doing it for centuries, Loren." I glanced at my blood-splattered coat. "Guess this'll be going to the cleaners. I'll get this, too," I said, slipping the handkerchief in my pocket.

Loren stood and sighed. "Well, I'll keep you posted on the goose and you keep me posted on you."

"I thought you were taking me out to lunch."

"Oh, change of plans," he said, clearing his throat. "We'll have to schedule a rain date."

"You're angry with me," I said.

"I'm in shock, Laura. I mean, your career is just taking off and now...."

"What?"

"The publisher isn't going to be none too pleased. You're a single woman, Laura."

"It's none of their business," I said.

"Well, try to keep it somewhat quiet, if you can."

"Quiet?" I said. "Loren, I'm not embarrassed about this. I'm so excited, I cannot stand it." I walked out, slamming his door and took an angry elevator ride down to the ground floor. *Why wasn't anyone happy for me?* Outside I was met by nasty, gusting wind. I wrapped my coat tightly around myself and went to the curb to hail a cab. Two pulled up and I opened the door to the first one.

"Laura?"

I turned to see Peter climb out of the other cab. He repeated my name, walking toward me with an odd expression.

I gripped the door handle. "You have to leave me alone, Peter," I said. "No more flowers, nothing."

His eyes skimmed over me, eyeing my bloodied coat. "You all right?"

I tottered, using the door for support. "I'm great. You have to honor the contract now."

He scowled. "You're bluffing."

"You'll have to trust me."

"Am I the father?"

"What do you think?"

"Laura, please, could we just go somewhere and talk?"

"Tempting, since I'm curious to know why you decided to stay here in the city."

"Okay, let's go someplace so I can explain."

I shook my head. "Forget it, but I'll be happy to have Mr. Pelton send you a copy of the contract you ripped up. You may need to be reminded what we agreed to." I then crawled into the back seat of the cab and shut the door, giving the driver my address.

"You're my first guest!" I lunged at Eric as he walked in, embracing him in a hug. Jenny was just behind him. She stiffened when I hugged her. "Come on in," I said.

"Sorry we're late," Eric said.

"No problem," I said. "Let's put your coats on the bed, then I'll give you the grand tour, which should take all of thirty seconds." Wordlessly, Eric and Jenny trailed behind me.

"I'm waiting for more of the furniture I ordered." I led them into my peaches-and-cream bedroom and tossed their coats on the bed. Jenny walked over to look out the window, but then glanced at the book on my nightstand. She went over and picked up my copy of *What Shall You Name Your Baby?*

"Let me show you the other rooms," I said. Jenny put the book down and followed me, but when I opened the door to the smaller bedroom and said, "This will be the nursery," she didn't look in, but dashed down the hallway toward the living room. Eric went after her, and I followed.

"I'm sorry," Jenny said, her bottom lip quivering. "It's just—"

Eric said, "We're not ready for this."

"I don't mean to be inconsiderate," I said. "I was just hoping I could at least talk about it with you."

Eric and Jenny didn't reply right away, but then Eric said, "Oh, this is for you." He handed me a gift.

I riffled through the tissue paper to find a crystal vase.

"We really didn't know what you needed," Jenny said.

"Oh, it's beautiful," I said, placing it on the coffee table. "Thank you." I headed into the kitchen. "I'll put the coffee on."

While I was scooping coffee grinds into the filter, Jenny walked in. She said, "Laura, I'm sorry."

"Don't be," I said. "It's just that I'm so happy, but can't seem to express it to anyone."

Eric walked in and not much later the three of us were sitting around the table with the coffee poured and crumb cake served.

"So," I said, "did you tell Beth, yet?"

Their forks in mid-air, their expressions wary, Eric and Jenny glanced at each other.

"We can't even talk about that?"

"That's not it," Eric said. "It's just she didn't take the news so well."

"I'm not surprised," I said. "What happened?"

Eric cleared his throat and rested his fork on his plate. "Beth is determined in her convictions. She's so stubborn."

"Don't I know it," I said.

He looked evenly at me. "That's one similarity you have with her." He took a sip of his coffee. "I went to see her on Monday night. Told her you were back. Then told her the rest." He looked down at his cup and didn't say anything for a moment.

"And…" I said.

Jenny rested her hand on his. "It's okay, honey."

He sucked up some air. "Laura," he said, "she's lost it."

"What do you mean?"

His eyes gazed far off.

"Eric?"

"Doesn't matter," he said. "Nothing good can come of it if I told you, anyway." His eyes filled with tears.

"Eric, what on earth did she say?'

Jenny said, "This has been so rough on him. Beth's been turning the church upside down with her personal crusade. She's—"

"Jenny, don't," Eric said.

"She's what?" I said.

Jenny hesitated, then said, "She's trying to get us ousted."

Eric refused to look at me.

"Because of me?" I said.

"Don't worry," Jenny said. "Most of the members are starting to see she's not quite right."

"But there are some on her side," Eric said, "all ranting about the sins of man."

"And using me as the prime example, right?"

"Eric has been doing his best to keep her from spilling the whole story," Jenny said.

"Until last Wednesday night," he said.

"What whole story?" I said.

"Everything," Jenny said, her voice trembling. "And now, since she found out that you were—" She hesitated and Eric patted her back. In measured tones, she continued. "Up till now she kept praising God for not blessing you. She was so sure He wouldn't let it happen." She shrugged. "Because it's not happening for us. And she said she's been praying for it not to happen for you. But when Eric told her you were pregnant, she did a complete turnaround."

Eric slammed his fist on the table, knocking coffee from our cups. "I tried to stop her, but this time...." He dropped his head in his hand.

The room was quiet. Eventually, in a whisper, Jenny said, "She said you sold your soul to the devil because there was no way the Lord would've permitted it."

"She said this in church?" I said. "In front of everyone?"

Eric nodded. "Including the caseworker."

"What caseworker?"

"The bank gave us a loan against the house so we could file for adoption. Mrs. Parker—the caseworker—wanted to see how established the church was so she came to service one night."

Jenny nodded, tears filling her eyes. "And there's Beth shouting that Eric was nothing but Judas because he wasn't censuring you."

"Doesn't matter anyway," Eric said. "The potential buyer we had backed out. The agency told us to come back when the house actually gets sold."

My throat became tight, my breathing labored.

"It was Jenny who somehow managed to calm Beth down," Eric said, while Jenny pushed crumbs around on her plate. "She walked over to Beth who was in the middle of ranting. Jenny put her arm around her and hugged her. It confused Beth enough to shut her up."

"She needs more than a hug, though," Jenny said. "We're all so worried about her, especially Don."

"Then Jenny suggested we pray."

I reached over to put my hand on Jenny's in gratitude, but the familiar odor stopped me. Deep scarlet blood began to splatter on to my blouse.

"Here!" Jenny handed me a wad of paper napkins.

"Pinch your nose," Eric said, standing over me, attempting to do it for me. When I had to exchange a blood-soaked napkin for a clean one for the third time, he suggested we call the doctor.

"No," I said. "It'll pass. It always does."

"This happens a lot?" Jenny said.

I shrugged. "Lots of weird things happen to a body during pregnancy." After several minutes went by, it was over. "I'm ruining more clothes this way," I said.

"Let's give your doctor a call, anyway," Eric said.

I waved him off. "I'm fine. And I'm hungry. Why don't we go down to Chinatown and eat our faces off. Ever have Peking duck?"

CHAPTER FIFTEEN

Laura

I tried to ignore the looks of disapproval and the unease I felt, but when the answering service told me that I had a call from Dr. Kim, I began to panic. "He wants you to call as soon as you get this message," I was told.

I edged down on my bed, my coat hanging from my shoulders. It took me several attempts to dial the numbers correctly. I huddled in my coat while the phone rang. And rang. Just as I was about to hang up, a voice said, "Dr. Kim's service."

I paused.

"Hello?"

"Uh, this is Laura Sumner." I hesitated, waiting for the gasp of privileged knowledge at the other end of the line. When there was none, I tried to sound untroubled. Still, my voice cracked when I said, "I'm returning Dr. Kim's call."

"This is his service. Is this an emergency?"

"Oh, no," I said, deciding to believe it so.

"If you give me your name and number, I'll give him your message when he calls in."

I told the officious voice I was actually returning the doctor's call and to let him know as much. I dropped the phone back in the cradle, slipped out of my coat, and went into the bathroom to take a shower.

I let the tepid water massage the muscles in my neck, work out the kinks. Then I took the bar of soap and circled it on my belly. What if there was no baby in there? What if that's what Dr. Kim needed to tell me? The water cascaded down my body. I poured shampoo in the palm of my hand, working the creamy liquid into my hair, rubbing it into lather. The water swirling down the drain was turning reddish brown. I credited it to rusty pipes, until

I wiped the soap from my face with my wash cloth and saw the blood.

It wasn't rust at all. I watched the bloody maelstrom swirl down the drain. The sight was familiar but suddenly frightening and, for some unexplained reason, I began to sob.

Turning one page after the next, I skimmed through a magazine. I watched Karen, the receptionist, but she kept her attention to answering the phone and paper work. I tried to discern from her demeanor the arcane information she may have about why I'd been summoned back before my scheduled appointment. The night before, Dr. Kim did return my call and told me to come in the following day.

"Is there a problem?" I'd said.

"We're going to discuss all that tomorrow in my office," he said.

"But—"

"One o'clock. See you then."

Now, by my watch, it was five minutes after one. Where the hell was he if it was so important? Mike would undoubtedly be annoyed that I wasn't at the staff meeting. I turned more magazine pages.

One-o-six. This was getting ridicu—

The door swung open and Dr. Kim flurried in. "Come with me," he said. Then, to Karen: "Hold all my calls."

I couldn't move, didn't want to. I was tempted to run the other way, if only I had the strength.

"Come in," Dr. Kim said, holding the door open for me. I put myself on autopilot and went in. He closed the door and went to his desk, motioning for me to sit.

"I want to admit you today," he said, sitting at his desk, an open folder in front of him.

"What's wrong?" I said, my body beginning to tremble.

"Well, we're going to determine all that."

"It's the baby. Something's wrong with my ba—"

"The baby's fine. It's you I'm concerned about."

"Me? I'm fine."

"How were you feeling before getting pregnant?"

"Before?" *Who remembers?*

"Tired?"

"Well, yeah, but I've been on tour and before that I just moved into my own place."

He leaned forward, looking me directly in the eyes. He paused. "Your white blood cell count is abnormal."

I thought about what he was saying and then relief washed over me. "You must've forgotten," I said, "but the lab tested my blood *before* I started taking the iron pills. I'm sure if you test it now...." I rolled up my sleeve. "Here, take some more. I've been taking those pills, so it should be—"

"Anemia is common with pregnancy. This isn't anemia."

"I probably need stronger pills."

He shook his head. "This is more serious. I want to admit you to confirm some of my suspicions. The doctor continued to talk, his mouth moving, but I didn't hear him. It had taken months to create the world I longed to be in and now it was falling piece by resounding piece all around me. From some distant place my name was being called.

"Do you hear me?"

I looked up to see the doctor's gaze focused on me. I nodded, but I hadn't really heard him at all.

The next three days rolled into one extended nightmare. Doctors with all sorts of foreign names examined me, but it was Dr. Kim who eventually walked into the hospital room, pulled up a chair. His expression was grim.

"All the results are back," he said, leafing through paperwork. "It's pretty much what I suspected."

I stared at him, my eyes filling with tears.

"You have what's known as CLL. Chronic lymphocytic leukemia."

The only word that I recognized was the last one. "So, what does that mean?" I said.

"It means we can't help you without harming the baby."

"Nothing is going to happen to my baby," I said.

"Well, you're my priority right now," he said.

"And the baby is mine." The room was closing in on me, my breathing becoming difficult.

"Then perhaps you shouldn't have put it in this situation. Or yourself."

I looked away.

"You need to make a decision," he said.

I didn't answer.

"This pregnancy seems to have exacerbated the disease. It's only going to continue doing so."

"No," I said.

"Laura, we're talking about saving your life."

"You don't understand what I went through to get her."

"Her?"

"It's a girl," I said, resting my hand on my abdomen.

"You don't know that."

"And I never would, if I let you do what you're suggesting."

Dr. Kim studied me for a moment, shuffling the papers in a neat pile. "I'm going to let you go home today. No work. Complete bed rest. You think about what I'm saying before you make a definite decision."

I shuffled into my apartment and turned up the thermostat.

"'bout time."

Startled, I turned to see that a familiar worn plaid easy chair was in my living room. I stared at the bald spot of the head just above the back of the chair. I faltered.

"Dad?"

"Thought you were going to hide forever."

"I ... I wasn't hiding." I circled to the front of the chair.

"Tryin' to punish her, huh?" He chuckled his sad chuckle.

I approached him. He wasn't looking at me, his glassy eyes staring off into some far away place. Hesitantly, I knelt at his feet. He had on his scruffy brown slippers.

"You give her a good fight," he said. "My tough girl." He patted me on the back. I winced in pain. How could he not feel the raised slashes?

"I don't know if I can fight this, Dad," I said, resting my head on his lap, eager for the comfort, but instead finding myself resting on my floral chintz cushion. The worn plaid easy chair had vanished.

"Dad?"

Beth hears voices. I talk to the dead.

I stumbled to my bedroom, the chill clinging to me, and crawled beneath the blankets while listening to the heat coursing through the radiators. I lie watching the gray press at my window. When I woke up some time later, I was still in my coat and the gray had turned to black. I turned on my lamp and picked up one of the pamphlets that was on my nightstand. It unfolded like a map with a fuzzy photograph of the developing baby in each of the nine squares. I studied the fourth square.

The baby was small and birdlike with distinguishable eyebrows distinctly marked. I began to trace the face with my finger, then retrace the outline, dipping down the barely perceptible nose.

I looked more closely. Was that an earlobe?

The phone rang. On the fifth ring, I picked it up.

"Laura, it's Beth."

My finger came to a halt at the tiny foot.

"I want you to come here on Sunday at three o'clock," she said. "To talk."

My finger zipped haphazardly around the curve of the head, then to the mouth where a thumb was plugged.

"Laura? You there?"

"To talk?" I said. "Why?"

"I figured one of us should end this cold war. It's the Christian thing to do."

The ninth square showed a fully formed baby. "Sunday?" I said.

"Yes, three o'clock."

A tear traveled down my face, landing on the head in the sixth square. "Okay," I said, then hung up. But if she was looking for a fight, I had none left.

CHAPTER SIXTEEN

Beth

I had about an hour before everyone was scheduled to arrive. I'm not sure if it was nervous energy, but I used the time to rake the fall leaves. The crisp air was invigorating and while I gathered the leaves into piles, I tried to talk to the Lord about what the day might bring. Sometimes the voices follow me, wedge their way into my head, but most times they stay in there—in the house—so I tried to approach Him while being under the autumn sky.

"Beth?"

I jumped and dropped the rake, but then realized it was Laura's voice and she was standing in the back yard. "You're early," I said, picking up the rake. "I said three o'clock."

"Does it really matter?"

It did, but I couldn't tell her why, otherwise she'd take off. "Well," I said, stalling for time, "let me just finish this." I began raking more leaves into a pile.

"Can't you talk and rake at the same time?" Laura trudged over and leaned against the maple tree.

"Not really," I said.

"So, did you get a buyer?"

I kept raking, trying not to look at her. Truth be told, we had several offers on the house, but then they changed their minds. "Not yet," I said. When Laura didn't reply, I looked up to see her touching a single leaf hanging to a skeletal branch. She didn't look too well, nothing like her fiery self. Guilt has a way of weighing on one's conscience and with the burden of shame she was carrying her weak spirit was understandable. I was hoping to change all that this afternoon.

"Beth, you said you wanted to talk."

I kept raking and said, "You don't make it easy. There's so much I want to say and I just don't know where to begin."

"I can guess what you want to say, Beth. It's no secret."

"Well, for one thing, I think it was real low of you to make Eric do your dirty work."

"My dirty work?"

"But I know why you didn't tell me yourself."

"Why's that?"

"Guilt. You know what you did was wrong." I picked up a plastic bag with one hand and tried to rake the leaves in with the other. It wasn't working. "Do you mind?" I brandished the bag at her.

She sucked up some air and came over, scooping up the leaves and shoving them in the bag. It was an act that knocked the wind out of her. The weight of sin, I suppose.

"Beth, I didn't do anything wrong. And nothing you say will make me believe otherwise."

How could that be? Are there different rules when you're sixteen? An illegitimate baby is an illegitimate baby. A sin. I said, "The Bible clearly sets the rules and if they are broken—"

She leaned far to one side, setting her sights alongside of me. I looked to see what she was staring at, but saw nothing. "What on earth are you doing?" I said.

"Looking for God."

"What?"

"I have you pegged to be on His right-hand side."

I pulled the bag from her grasp. "You are so irreverent."

"I guess," she said. "You would think Mom and her spare-the-rod-spoil-the-child whippings would've curbed all that."

"She was following the word of God, Laura."

"Well, we certainly weren't spoiled, damaged is more like it." Her voice quivering, she said, "Is that what did it for you, Beth? Was it simply easier to surrender than fight?"

I twisted the bag and closed it in a knot. "I thank God that she loved me enough to … to raise me in the way I should go. I'll get to heaven now for that."

"But why'd she have to put us through hell to get there?" Then, barely above a whisper, she said, "Can't we just make it okay between us, Beth?"

I stopped and studied her. Maybe she was having a change of heart. I said, "I'd like that."

She had a barely perceptible smile. "I'd like it if we could just laugh as sisters one more time."

"What do you mean?"

"I remember when I used to beg you and Eric to play Ring-around-the Rosie with me."

I leaned on the rake, the memory flooding back to me. I had forgotten that we'd ever been children, doing children things.

"And each time we say, 'we all fall down,' we would fall on top of each other...."

"Laughing so hard, we'd cry," I said, giving the memory a voice.

"Just kids helping each other up off the ground so that we could do it all over again." Her eyes filled with tears. "Help me, Beth."

The rake slipped from my grasp. "What on earth?"

"I'm sick."

"Well go lay down!"

"No, that's not what I mean. I'm really sick."

"So you're not going to have a—"

"Yes, but—"

She then began to spill her story, about how she was very ill. She said something about blood and cancer, but then stopped talking. There was silence between us until she added, "This is where you tell me it'll be all right, that I'll get through it."

I took a step closer. "Don't you see, Laura? It all makes perfect sense. This is God trying to get your attention. He's trying to get you to repent."

She gazed at me without saying anything. Then I heard the long-awaited car doors slamming. They'd arrived! I raced into the house to turn on the coffee urn. I was sure her illness would now make it easier to get her to listen to reason. Praise Jesus. Sometimes someone needs to be knocked down to the ground in order for righteousness to pick them back up. Laura trailed in after me.

"You expecting company?" she said.

"Yes, we just want to talk to you," I said.

The doorbell rang and I ran to open the front door to find Mary and a group of women waiting. I explained that Laura had arrived earlier than expected. "Sit down," I said, running back to the kitchen. The urn was sighing and sputtering, but there was no Laura. I ran into the backyard, but she wasn't there either. When I ran around to the front of the house the Thunderbird was pulling from the curb and driving away.

Eric

I slid onto the vinyl seat and huddled against the window. The train conductor's muffled, intercomed voice announced successive stops, ending with Penn Station—my destination. It was a forty minute ride. I would use the time to sort out all that had happened.

I'd called Laura the night before, moments after Beth made her dreadful announcement. Her voice resigned, Laura confirmed that Beth was telling the truth. Morning followed a long, sleepless night. I stumbled around the house looking for my car keys, patting pockets, riffling papers on the counter and snapping at Jenny in the confusion. It was Jenny who suggested I take the train.

"You're too upset to drive," she said, her face tracked with tears.

Finally, the keys were found in the blankets of the unmade bed and Jenny drove me to the station. She kept asking if I wanted her to come with me, but I needed time alone with my sister.

With my knuckles pressed into my chin, I stared out the window as the train pulled out of Seabrook and headed toward Manhattan. I felt as if I were about to snap—a rent here, a gash there, splitting me into tiny shreds of a man. For that, I have Beth to thank.

Sunday evening service began routinely enough. It's always been my favorite service.

"Jesus is the Rock," someone called out and everyone would join in singing while Douglas would pound the piano keys. Then someone else would shout out another hymn, and after several were sung, I'd suggest it was time for sharing. I call Sunday evening the 'good news service' because it was a time set aside for praise and thanks, unlike Wednesday evenings when we focused on burdens.

"I have something to share," Beth said, leaping to her feet.

I never know what to expect from her anymore, so I said, "Remember our intention here."

"Well, I came across some Bible verses today that I'd like to share, if that's okay with you, Pastor."

You can't stop someone from wanting to quote the Bible on any night of the week, so I gave her a nod of approval.

First, she flipped the Bible open to Deuteronomy, recited a verse, then moved to Samuel. While leafing through the pages, she reminded the congregation how much our mother loved to quote those verses. It made sense to me because they all conveyed the same message of the repercussions of sin. Eventually, I had to interrupt her and ask if she were close to being finished.

"Here's the last one I'll share tonight," she said. "It's from Proverbs." And she went on to recite: "A good man obtaineth favor of the Lord: but a man of wicked devices will He condemn." With the Bible resting in her arms, she looked around the congregation, and said, "I take great comfort that the Lord keeps His promises."

"Amen!" Mrs. Tregette shouted.

"Laura should've listened," she said.

I took a step toward Beth, exchanging glances with Jenny.

"If she had, she wouldn't be punished for her defiance."

Town after Long Island town whirred by, but I was once again standing in the church in front of the congregation.

"Some of you know that she was at my house today."

That was news to me.

"I invited her so I could give her another chance. You know, turn the other cheek and all. But before we even got the opportunity to talk she tells me that she's dying."

I can't say for sure what I was feeling then. I suppose I was too shocked to feel much. And doubtful about what Beth was saying. Because I couldn't speak, Beth had the advantage and began sermonizing that the church had a responsibility to take heed to the lesson. While she compared Laura with

Lot's wife, Don rose from his seat and instructed Beth to sit down. Then he told me to go call my sister, see if any of what Beth was saying was true.

"I'll keep things running here," he said.

Before Beth had a chance to turn Laura into a pillar of salt, I was out the door.

Maybe, I hoped, maybe Don was right. Maybe none of what Beth said was true. She was becoming more unbalanced everyday and maybe she'd finally snapped. Maybe. But I was fighting the memory of how wan Laura appeared the last few months and there was that sickening relentless nose bleed.

At some point I reached the parsonage. I hadn't realized that Jenny followed me, but she dialed Laura's number and handed me the receiver just as my sister picked up. I sank into myself when Laura confirmed the news. When I hung up, Jenny threw her arms around me and we clung to each other, sobbing.

"Penn Station."

The train rumbled out of the dark tunnel and into the fluorescent terminal. I got up from my seat and made my way through the crowd of hustling commuters.

When I reached Laura's apartment, it took her forever to disengage the lock. Not waiting for her to open the door, I pushed my way in. Immediately, she assumed some sort of pleasantry in true Laura fashion, but I pulled her into my arms, my body shuddering against her limp, tiny frame.

A moment later, she pushed away. "Okay, okay," she said, barely above a whisper.

I pulled a crumpled handkerchief from my coat pocket and wiped my eyes.

"You're getting to be some city slicker, aren't you?" she said, walking into the living room.

"I don't mind it here. Just can't deal with all the congestion."

"That's what makes it Manhattan," she said, gesturing for me to sit. I couldn't move though; couldn't stop looking at her.

"Why don't you take your coat off? I'll make you some coffee."

"I don't want coffee." I walked over and dropped down on to the couch. "This, this thing you got...."

"Crazy, isn't it?"

"But you're still pregnant?" I wasn't sure if one had anything to do with the other.

She nodded.

"So, what's being done to help you, to fight it?"

She shrugged. "Not much. Not for now. Once I have the baby, then they can begin treatments."

"But you told Beth that you were...."

"Some days I think I am," she said. "Funny how I can't refute what Beth thinks."

"What do you mean?"

"You know."

"How God punishes us?"

She nodded, tears coming to her eyes. I thought of all the counseling that I did, of all the faithless husbands who hide in my office confessing their transgressions, of the young boy who cannot find it in his heart to like girls, of the housewife who likes to drink brandy until she can no longer function. I said, "Do you believe that?"

"I don't know what to believe."

I looked around her apartment. For the most part, it was cold and bare, except for the couch and coffee table. There were no pictures on the wall. She was so alone, but I guess in reality she'd always been. That's when a thought occurred to me. "Laura, where's that English fellow?"

"Doesn't matter," she said.

"Doesn't matter? He has a responsibility here, Laura!"

She shook her head. "No, he doesn't. I made sure of that."

I wasn't certain what she meant and my expression must have revealed as much.

"You wouldn't understand."

"Did you love him?"

She didn't reply.

"Did he love you?"

She shrugged. "I wouldn't know."

"Man, she really did something to you, didn't she?"

"Who?"

"Mom."

She sniffed. "I didn't try to be difficult, Eric. I learned all those verses, too. Up here," she said, pointing to her head. "But they weren't real to me. I didn't feel them here." She placed a fist over her heart. "I just felt empty. That's when I was sure that God turned His back on me. And if a mother and God can't love me, well, who could?"

There'd been a time that I thought it was Laura who'd been the one to have conquered the harm done to us by Mother. I shifted over and pulled my sister against me. I wanted to carry her burdens, her tears, her loneliness, leaving her to be the brilliant woman I believe she is.

"I'm not going to lose you," I said. "We'll get you well."

"You believe that?" she said.

"With all my heart. It's called faith, Laura."

CHAPTER SEVENTEEN

Laura

"Where the hell you been?"

I looped around Mike, ignoring the veins popping out on his bright red forehead and went straight to my office with him right behind me.

"You don't call, don't show up, or even beam me the goddamn column! And now you're acting like I'm the one who fucked up! This is bullshit."

I started gathering my papers, considered what to do with them, and then tossed them in the wastebasket.

"Someone please remind me to never let my wife get pregnant. This mood crap is plain bullshit."

"I'm sorry, but I have to take a leave of absence. Doctor's orders."

Mike hesitated. He studied me for a minute while I took a folded sheet of paper from my pocket.

"It's all here," I said. "It explains everything. There's even a doctor's note."

Scowling, he took the note from me. "Listen, if you have to stay in bed, fine. You can write your column from home. I'll send Bobby to come over and pick it up."

"No," I said. "I won't have the strength. I'm sorry to do this, you know, resigning while giving you only a...," I forced a smile. "... day's notice. I always wanted to say that."

A few days later returning from Dr. Kim's, the taxi pulled up to my building and I spotted Loren talking to the doorman. Not a good sign. I paid the fare and climbed out. It wasn't easy to read him, but I could tell he knew, some-how, he knew; his face was the same ashen color as his hair.

"We need to talk," he said. "Can we go up?"

It wasn't until we got to my apartment and sat down that I asked how he knew.

"Called the paper," he said. "Your column's been missing for a couple of weeks now."

"You read my column?"

"Yeah, I read your column."

"So, Mike told you."

"What he knows. Still doesn't answer the hundreds of questions I have."

"Join the club." I'd just finished trying to ask the doctor some of those questions.

"How sick are you?"

"Enough to think that there may not be a Pink Goose series."

Loren sighed. "It's not right. None of it is. And you having to deal with this all alone. How 'bout we get the father involved?"

It was tempting, but I'd signed a contract promising neither to bother him nor ask for help. No matter what. Go figure. "I can't, Loren," I said, fearful I'd blurt Peter's name. "We have an agreement."

"So, he knows?"

"That I'm pregnant? Yeah."

"What about the other thing."

"That I'm sick?" I shook my head. "Doesn't matter."

He rubbed his chin. "None of this makes sense, Laura. What can I do?"

"Nothing."

"I don't buy that. There's gotta be some way I can help."

"Well, yeah."

"Name it."

"Could you get me off the hook for anymore promoting right now?"

"Absolutely. Anything you want."

Low, rumbling voices and the aroma of turkey roasting woke me up. It took a moment for me to remember that I was on the cot in Jenny's sewing room and it was Thanksgiving morning. The night before Eric came into Manhattan to pick me up so that I could spend the holiday with them.

I wasn't ready to get up yet and lay quietly with one hand on the swell of my belly. It had been about a week ago that I'd felt the baby move for the first time. It was no more than a flutter, but now I spend hours waiting for the sensation to reoccur. It's a hopeful reminder that there is life in me. Right now, though, I felt nothing.

In measured movements, I sat up and swung my feet to the side of the cot. After several more minutes went by, I pushed myself up and shuffled over to the window. It looked to be a cold gray day. Across the street, I watched a leaf gambol across the church lawn until it was out of sight.

There was a light rap on the door. "Laura? You okay?"

"I'm fine, Jenny," I said. "I'll be out in a few minutes."

"No rush. I was just wondering—"

"I'm okay." I tried to confirm it by running a brush through my hair and pinching my cheeks for color. I walked out into the kitchen.

"Good morning, dear," Jenny's mother said. She was sitting at the table peeling potatoes. "I hope you slept well. Jenny feels badly about putting you on the cot, but I told her we'd take the upstairs since you shouldn't be climbing those steps."

"I slept fine," I said.

"Did you take your medicine?"

"Mom…," Jenny said, looking up from the dough she was rolling out, her face dusty with flour.

"I'm supposed to eat something first," I said.

"Oh, let me make you some eggs." Jenny dropped the rolling pin and rushed to the refrigerator.

"No, no. Toast is fine. I'll get it." I headed to the counter, intercepted by Jenny.

"One or two slices?"

I rested my hand on her arm. "Jenny, please don't feel you have to wait on me. It's just toast."

Her expression was a mix of frustration and worry, but she backed away and let me take two slices of bread out of the bag and put them in the toaster. "Where's Eric?" I said.

"Over at the church with my dad." Jenny was back at the table pounding another lump of dough. "He'll be back soon."

I took a chair at the table. Jenny's mom pressed her brown cow-eyes on me. After a moment's hesitation, she reached over and placed her hand on mine, her fingers brown from the potatoes. "I just want you to know how terrible I feel about everything. We're praying for you, you know. For you to get healed."

I nodded.

"Even if you are not married, we still—"

"Mom!" Jenny said.

Her mother pulled her hand away and went back to peeling the potatoes, her lips pursed.

The toaster popped and I stood back up.

"There's orange juice," Jenny said.

"Thanks," I said. After pouring myself a glass and fixing my toast, I said, "Mind if I take this inside and watch the parade?"

"Oh, not at all. There's supposed to be a pink goose float, right?"

"Balloon," I said.

"Call me when it comes on, okay?"

I went into the living room and flicked on the television. The parade had already started. I hoped I hadn't missed my goose. With a couch spring poking me in the back, I sipped my juice and chewed on dry toast while watching some celebrity I didn't recognize sing some syrupy rendition of "Frosty the Snowman." Once she was finished, the float she was on jerked her out of view and a high school band performed a jazzy Jingle Bells.

"How you doing?" Eric walked in and settled down next to me.

"Good," I said.

"I don't know if Jenny told you or not, but Beth won't be coming over today."

That was news to me. "Why?"

"She's cooking; invited some people over from church."

Snoopy was floating over the Manhattan crowd, his ears flapping in the wind. "How's she doing?"

He shook his head. "Not great. We're really worried about her."

Just then, floating onto the small television screen, a mammoth pink goose appeared. I gasped, bringing my hand to my mouth. Eric called everyone into the living room.

"Isn't that nice?" Jenny's mom said. Jenny and her father mumbled in agreement.

Then, almost as quickly as it appeared, the goose was off the screen.

"That was just great," Eric said, tapping my knee. "I'm going to help Jen, but you let us know if you need anything."

"So, this tiny Filipino lady comes chasing after me with a frying pan that's about the same size she is," Jenny's dad was saying, his ruddy face getting ruddier as he went on. "Now I'm trying to escape down this narrow alley, but she's a quick one."

Eric and Jenny were howling while Jenny's mother kept using her napkin to wipe tears of laughter from her eyes. I smiled, ladling gravy into the craters I'd made in my mashed potatoes.

"Well," Jenny's mom said, "it wasn't until later that we found out when your father was trying to invite her to Sunday service, by trying to speak the language, he must have implied something rather awful. He was lucky to get away from her and that pan."

"She sure was a spitfire," Jenny's dad said. "After that, I didn't try to speak Filipino to anyone until I was absolutely certain I knew what I was saying."

Between laughter and conversation, the turkey was carved to the bone and the stuffing scraped clean from the bowl. Now forks and knives rested on our plates and everything seemed to have come to a post-dinner lull.

Jenny's dad patted his paunch. "I'm never going to be able to budge from this table."

"Oh, yes you are," Jenny's mom said, poking him with her elbow. She pushed back her chair and stood. "We're going for a walk."

"A walk! I can't even move."

"Yes, you can," she said, tapping him on the shoulder. He scowled at her, a toothpick propped in his mouth. "I think now would be a good time for a walk," she said, staring him down.

"Oh! Oh yeah," he said. "A walk; I could use the exercise."

There was a sudden change in the room, the atmosphere turning somber. Eric and Jenny didn't move and we all sat watching as her parents slipped on their coats while making forced small talk about the wonders of a crisp stroll after such a heavy meal. Before Jenny's mom went out the door, I saw her look pointedly at Jenny and clasp her hands in an attitude of prayer. They closed the door and the house took on a peculiar, uncomfortable silence. I reached for my plate, but Jenny went to stop me.

"I'm okay, Jenny," I said. "I function very well."

Eric cleared his throat. "We know, Laura. It's just that there's something we'd like to talk to you about."

I put the plate back down and looked from Eric to Jenny, their expressions tentative.

"It's awfully difficult to know where to begin," Eric said.

"You don't need to say anything," I said, "Just be my brother and leave the preacher side out of this."

"I wasn't going to preach to you, Laura," Eric said. "We wanted to talk to you about, well, the baby."

Jenny bit her lip and Eric picked up a fork, tapping it on the table. "We're so heartbroken about this ... this disease you have. It's a tragedy. We don't see it as anything else." He coughed. "But." He faltered. "I don't mean, but. I mean, you seem to be handling all this incredibly well, and I sincerely find that commendable."

Commendable?

"But it's going to get more difficult for you. You're going to need help."

"You're welcome to stay with us," Jenny said.

"Thank you," I said, "but my doctor wants to admit me in a few weeks. He says he has to keep a close eye on everything."

Eric said, "But once you begin the treatments, who's going to take care of the baby?"

"I am," I said.

"You're going to be too sick," Jenny said. "You're going to need help."

"Jenny, it was my faith that got me pregnant and that same faith is going to get me through this."

"But you should be prepared, you know, have things decided before—"

"Before what, Jenny? Before I die?"

She went white and Eric mumbled, "We're not saying that."

"Really? Because it certainly sounds like it. I don't plan to give up my baby."

"We're just offering you help," Eric said. "The chemo is going to wipe you out. The side effects are horrendous. I mean, remember how sick Mom was? Just walking from the bathroom to the bedroom exhausted her."

"That's because she was dying, Eric. I'm not dying."

"Laura, Dr. Kim is very concerned—"

"How do you know Dr. Kim?"

Eric and Jenny glanced warily at each other.

"You called my doctor?" I said. "Why?"

"No, he called us. He's worried. He doesn't think you understand just how serious this is."

I stared at them. "This explains a lot," I said. "There was no need to push your parents out for a walk in this weather."

"We care about you," Eric said.

"I think it's something else. I think this is about my baby, about your wanting my baby."

"Stop it," Eric said.

"You believe I'm going to die." I rested my hand on my abdomen. "And I have what you want."

"I said stop it!" Eric jumped up, his chair crashing to the floor.

The kitchen door creaked open. Jenny's parents crept into the living room, their faces red from the cold. After surveying the fallen chair, Jenny's tear-filled eyes and Eric's angry stance, Jenny's mother said, "Why don't we go upstairs for a little while?"

"That's not necessary," I said. "We're done here. I think I'll lie down for awhile." I got up, making my way past all their eyes watching my trembling self leave the room.

Moments later, I lay curled on the cot, my fist jammed in my mouth to muffle the sobs. Accusations echoed round in my head. I tried to quiet them and let the memory of Peter's voice comfort me. I hadn't realized I'd fallen asleep until a persistent tap startled me awake. I gasped for air, finding myself surrounded in darkness. There was a space of time where I thought I was gone, no more, until the door opened and light washed into the room from the hallway.

"You okay?" Jenny said.

"I guess. I must've slept for awhile."

"Through dessert and most of the football game." She came in and sat next to me on the cot, the springs squeaking. "You're wrong, you know."

I lay quietly, unable to speak.

"We care about you, Laura. We aren't trying to take anything from you."

"It's this baby that's going to keep me alive, Jen."

"I hope so," Jen said. "Eric and I both hope so."

"You know, I'm just starting to understand what having faith really means," I said.

"Good," Jenny said. "Maybe you can teach me." When I didn't reply, she said, "Eric will take you home now, if you're ready."

"I'm ready."

Street lamps arced over the road, lighting the path along the parkway. A flurry or two fluttered in the headlights while a barely visible dusting covered the path back to the city. Eric drove fast enough to make the car shimmy. I wanted to ask him to slow down, but he seemed more intent on getting me home than hearing anything I had to say.

The silence lasted for much of the ride, the flurries evolving into a snowstorm. We came to a sharp curve in the highway and the car skidded from the left lane into the right. I covered my mouth, but it was too late to stifle my scream. Without a word, Eric let the wheels straighten themselves and drove on. What if I shattered on impact? I felt fragile enough to do so. The unexpected touch of Eric's hand on mine made me jump.

"You okay?" he said,

Tears began to stream down my face.

"I have it under control. See," he said, "both hands on the wheel."

"Just don't hate me, Eric," I said.

"I don't hate you," he said.

"But you're angry with me."

"Yeah, I am. And I'm hurt."

I stared ahead, the flakes mesmerizing me, the road turning into a sheet of white.

CHAPTER EIGHTEEN

Laura

It was five days before Christmas, but instead of festooning garland from the archway and deciding where the tree should go, I was closing up shop: Dr. Kim said it was time to admit me. He'd tried to make the dreary situation sound cheerful by saying, "Pregnant women are supposed to be pampered."

I wriggled into my wool coat before noticing the bedraggled bouquet of flowers that were on the coffee table. They were a gift from Day's Notice. I debated leaving them, but then changed my mind and carried the vase off to the kitchen, dumping the flowers into the garbage. I then poured the slimy water down the drain, washed the vase and left it to dry on the drain board.

The refrigerator's hum caught my attention. I opened the door and scanned the contents on the bright shelves. The half-carton of milk and unfinished tin of baked ziti would be history by the time I returned. Using the sink for support, I poured the milk down the drain, then tossed out the carton, along with the leftovers. I then took a final stroll through the apartment, stopping at the nursery. The rocking chair was sitting in the corner and a bassinet was set up with fresh sheets. I didn't have much else ready, though, and began to panic with the thought. I was already failing as a mother.

I went back into the living room and grabbed my duffle bag. I turned the thermostat down, but then immediately turned it back up. The apartment would need to be warm when I brought my baby home. I wandered into the hall and locked the door behind me. I went to the elevator and when I reached the lobby, Paul hailed me a cab.

"Sloane-Kettering," I told the driver, but when he clicked on the meter and pulled into the street, I said, "Would you mind taking me over to St. Patrick's first? I'll only be a few minutes."

The taxi raced down Fifth Avenue and it wasn't long before I spotted the cathedral's spires. The driver pulled into a No Standing Zone and I told him to keep the meter running and climbed out. I followed a stream of people in through the doors and soon stood in a center aisle, miles from the majestic altar. I was surrounded by people gazing in awe at the lofty craftsmanship. I walked past the statues while refracted light poured in from the stained-glass windows, bathing everything in a golden haze. There were attitudes of reverence, no one speaking above a whisper. Column after column was adorned with a wreath for the holiday. I walked until I reached a roped off section, the intention appearing to keep the public from close proximity to the altar. Approaching God here was not simply a matter of bowing one's head and petitioning Him. No. Here it was obvious one must be prepared before entering the realm of His glory. I gazed up, wishing for the face of God to appear, the bombastic voice to summon me forward in order to account for my presence. I wasn't familiar with the God who dwelled here and turned to observe those around me.

One shriveled woman was scrunched down in the pew and on her knees, her face hidden in her folded arms. A low whisper came from her as her crooked fingers moved along a string of beads draped over spotted hands.

Next to a stand of votive candles, the flames flickering in the dim light, stood a man who looked to be about sixty. Garbed in a suit, he was holding a hat in his hands and rotating it by the rim. I moved closer to get a better view, perhaps to hear what he was saying to the statue set back in the vaulted wall. Its marble face was gazing down on him with pity. The man stopped and turned, his brown eyes sweeping over me with cool reserve. I backed away and walked further down the aisle until I noticed a life-size nativity tucked in the corner. No one was supplicating the Christ child just then, so I dropped down to my knees and leaned on the railing that corralled the manger. There was a bed of musty straw that created an earthy tableau. I paid little heed that Mary's eyes were a painter's handiwork and tried to find something in them as they gazed beatifically at the ceramic infant.

The image of the old woman hunched over, her crippled fingers manipulating the string of beads came to mind. Then there was the man, twirling his hat while imploring a block of chiseled marble. How long had they been coming here, hoping to be heard? Had there been a sign that caused them to return, time and time again?

I never prayed to anything but empty space before and that had been years ago. Now, I pressed my eyes closed and worked myself up to dare approach whomever was listening. It took a moment to visualize Jesus, mentally focusing on his face, not that of the babe in the manger, but the benign, radiant savior's face of an artist's rendering. I pleaded for his help.

Then I recalled the statue—graven image as it was—and prayed it would listen to me.

Now, the flickering votive candles, willing the flames to reach the heavens and demand His attention.

And those prayer beads. I'd get myself some and chant, if it meant delivering me from this horrid nightmare.

It's not death I fear. No, I'd welcome it for the answers alone. My grief is from having to leave behind what I had purposely conceived, desperately yearned.

Just then there was a stirring inside me. I placed a hand on my swollen belly. I was ready to go on in prayer when something told me to be quiet. And believe.

I was quiet.

I believed.

I waited for a miracle.

My eyes closed, I remained still, wondering how I'd know when it happens. I rested my head on the railing.

Or was I expected to go in faith?

How much time passed, I couldn't be sure, but at some point I lifted my head. Mary's stony face came into focus, looking complacently down at the baby with the outstretched arms. I turned to see the sunlight stream through the stained-glass windows. The old woman was gone, as was the man with the hat.

It was time for me to go, too.

I pushed myself up from the kneeler and took the long, slow walk back to the waiting taxi with the meter ticking.

"Merry Christmas."

I opened my eyes to see Eric and Jenny standing in the doorway. I pushed myself up into a sitting position and invited them in. They approached the bed as if uncertain what I'd say or do. I hadn't seen them since Thanksgiving. Eric had a present in his hand.

"How's it going?" I said.

Eric's eyes filled with tears. "We were wrong not to come before this."

"I know you talk to my doctors," I said. "They tell me."

Eric nodded. Then, as if he just realized he was holding the present, he placed it on my lap and wished me a Merry Christmas again.

"You shouldn't have done this," I said. "I don't have anything for you."

"We weren't expecting anything," Jenny said. "Go on, open it."

I ripped off the paper decorated with gleeful Santas and pulled out a flannel nightgown sprinkled with tiny pink roses. "Oh, this is lovely," I said. *Lovely,* a word I never use.

"I guess it's more my taste," Jenny said. "I can exchange it, if you want."

"No, no," I said, perhaps a bit too adamantly. "I'm getting tired of these sweats myself." I put the nightgown in the box and set it on the nightstand next to my bed.

"So, how are you feeling?" Eric said, dropping into a chair at the foot of the bed.

"Eager to get out of here. I have so many things I need to do. I don't really have many things for the baby; she's going to need diapers and pajamas."

"She?" Jenny said.

"I just know it's a girl," I said.

Jenny walked to the window, keeping her back to me.

"They have it decorated nicely." Eric pointed at the bit of garland over the door and the tiny plastic tree on the nightstand.

"That's Maggie's doing. She's the night nurse. She welcomed Christmas with me last night."

Eric nodded, glancing at Jenny's back.

"So," I said, "how's Beth doing?"

"Oh," Eric said, "okay. She sends her love."

"No, she doesn't," I replied.

Jenny turned around. "You're right, Laura. She doesn't."

"Jen—"

"Eric, why do you keep covering for her?" Jenny looked at me. "We want her to get help, but she won't listen. The Realtor won't even bring anyone to the house anymore. It's a waste of time. Eric keeps making excuses for her."

He rubbed his eyes. "I don't have the energy for her anymore."

"But you need the money for the house," I said.

"Hellooo...."

Loren and his wife Esther appeared in the doorway. "Oh, sorry," Esther said, "we didn't know you had company already. We'll come back."

"That's not necessary," Eric said, standing. He shook Loren's hand. "We'll go get some coffee and be back in a bit." He and Jenny went out the door, promising to return shortly.

"I hope we didn't chase them away," Esther said.

"No, you were probably the excuse they needed."

"Well, glad they finally came around," Loren said, placing a large rectangular box adorned with a big red bow on my lap. It weighed hardly anything.

"What's this?" I said.

"Open it and see."

I lifted the cover off and could do nothing but stare.

"She must like it," Loren said. "She's speechless."

"He didn't want you to know about it," Esther said. "Isn't it just wonderful?"

I lifted a stuffed pink goose from the box. My pink goose. I caressed the downy soft feathers. "Wow. This is amazing."

"I think it could be a big seller," Esther said.

"So, do we have your permission to market it?" Loren said.

"I get a percentage out of it?"

"Absolutely," he said.

I nodded. "Yeah, you got my permission."

"This is going to keep the book moving," Loren said.

I settled back on my pillow, forcing my eyes to stay open, ignoring the discomfort as best as I could.

"Laura, you okay?" Loren said.

I nodded.

Esther walked over and began caressing my hair. "We wish we could do something for you."

It was as if I were on another plane, my eyes refusing to open, my mouth saying things over which I had little control. Peter's image came to mind. I mumbled, "Just tell him I'm sorry when you see him."

Their voices grew distant. Then, two gentle kisses brushed my cheek. With one hand on my belly, the other resting on the pink goose, I drifted off.

CHAPTER NINETEEN

Laura

The month was March. Dr. Kim tucked the stethoscope in his pocket and placed the chart back at the foot of my bed. He drew a chair up alongside of me and sat down. He sighed, "I think the baby's big enough now to survive outside the womb."

"Really?" I said, my heart pounding with excitement.

"I want to induce labor."

"Okay," I said. "When?"

"Well, it's more complicated than that."

"You've induced labor before, right?"

"Not with someone in your condition." He cleared his throat. "I need to ask you something."

I turned my head, looking out the window.

"What arrangements have you made for the baby?"

"I take her home, feed her. Change her diapers." *Love her. Watch her grow.*

"Laura...."

"What do you want me to say?"

"Who'll be caring for her?"

"Me," I said, my throat closing up, tears streaming down my face.

"You're not going to be strong enough. Think about it and we'll talk again tomorrow."

Later that night, at an hour when the hall was free from clattering carts and the nurses' chatter had decreased to a passing murmuring, I climbed out of bed and scuffed over to the window. The streets below were sluggish, silenced by the hour. A single patch of dirty snow remained on the sidewalk. Winter had its opportunity, now spring was emerging. After being holed up in the hospital for the long depressing season, I was ready to live again. With the birth of my baby fast approaching, I believed it to be possible.

I sat down in what had become Eric's chair. Since the New Year, he and Jenny visited almost daily. They never brought the subject up of taking the baby again. Eric would sometimes rush into the room carrying articles from medical books about how certain diseases can be cured with alternative medicines. He'd wait for Dr. Kim to appear and implore him to consider them. Other times, Eric would pace around the room and read from "The Lion, the Witch and the Wardrobe" and affect Aslan's orotund, majestic voice, making me laugh out loud. Then something would make him stop reading and he would flash a strange, perhaps dismal look he sometimes gives me and his eyes would tear up.

Then there were the times he would see I was feeling down. Hesitantly, he'd take the Bible he'd put in my nightstand drawer and ask if I'd mind if he read. I didn't. As a matter-of-fact, something in his voice calmed me. He'd sit in his chair by the window and often read from Psalms. While he went on about green pastures and still waters, I'd close my eyes and massage the hill of my belly, imagining what it would be like when the nightmare ends.

A sudden twinge tightened in my abdomen and I reached over, grabbing onto the windowsill. I tried to breathe steadily and waited for it to pass. Finally, it did and I sat back in the chair, recalling the days that Jenny visited when Eric could not.

The first few times she stole into the room, her face blanched and tense, her purse clenched in her hands. When it was time to leave, she studied the train schedule. I would highlight the departure time and told her over and over again where to ask for the track number. But, as the weeks passed, she began jaunting into the room, her purse swinging at her side.

"Five today," she'd say, dropping a shopping bag loaded with games and her sketch pad on a chair. "Five men whistled at me and I did what you told me to do each time. Didn't even look their way, just kept my head up as if they were invisible."

I laughed.

"But…," she said.

"What?"

"Well," she said, "is it wrong to sort of like the attention?"

I laughed and said, "Not at all." How refreshing she'd become.

Eric and Jenny seldom mentioned Beth to me anymore, but when I asked about her, I detected their pain. They told me it was better if I didn't hear everything that she was up to. Perhaps it's better that she doesn't visit or call, yet I admit that it hurts she doesn't want to see me.

But these weren't the thoughts that kept me awake. Instead, it was what Dr. Kim had implied earlier. Decide on an alternative plan. Choose is what he was saying.

I began to shake uncontrollably with another sudden twinge.

Me. I choose me!

Queasiness came upon me, my body trembling from a cold sweat.

If I were to choose someone, that would mean I was giving up. How could I give up?

The room began to whirl, as if I were being twirled by a dancing fool.

I couldn't give up.

Pain, sharp and relentless, seized me. I called out to the night nurse: "Maggie!"

Eric

DOESN'T MATTER HOW MANY PAINTINGS OF IRISES THERE ARE or the brightness of the walls, a waiting room feels like a waiting room with time suspended from one anxious moment to the next. Dr. Kim had called the night before to tell us that Laura had gone into early labor. Jenny and I hurried as quickly as we could, but by the time we got to the hospital, Laura had given birth to a baby girl. Laura had been right all along, except now she was in critical condition and all we wanted was for her to wake up. We were counting on it. With faith.

I'd called Beth from the hospital to let her know that she was an aunt.

"Not me," she said. "Not to that baby." Then she hung up.

I also called Loren to give him the news. Both he and Esther were now with Jenny and me, each taking turns, pacing, holding cups of coffee that turned cold. Every once in awhile one of us would take a stroll to the nursery and gaze at the tiny pink bundle. Each time I looked at that baby girl, my prayer was for her mother to see her, to hold her. Dr. Kim doesn't think she'll be able to do much beyond that. But I tell myself that Dr. Kim is a man of science and does not live by the same faith I do.

Loren sat down beside me, the two of us looking up at the TV screen with images coming from Memphis with Dr. King leading a march that suddenly broke out in a riot. What a world in which to bring in a baby.

"How you holding up?" Loren said.

I shook my head. "Been better."

"She'll fight it," he said. "She's David to this darn Goliath."

I glanced at him.

He shrugged. "Trying to talk your lingo."

I laughed. "Not necessary. Dad thought the world of you and so does Laura, that's enough for me. And I know what you're saying."

Loren's eyes made it to the TV screen. "When I think of that little girl, I wonder what's going to happen to her," he said. "Just wish I knew where the father was. He needs to know what's going on."

"Probably back in England by now," I said.

Loren turned, staring at me as if I'd said something profound. "You know him?"

"Met him once. An Englishman, some writer."

Loren jumped up. "Esther, you hear this?"

Esther put down her magazine. "What?"

"Eric knows who the father is."

I looked over at Jenny. "Peter somebody, right?"

She nodded. "I don't know his last name, though."

"Peter!" Loren said, his eyes wide. He patted his pockets for what I assume was his keys and yelled at Esther to come along. They were out the door in a flash.

Jenny and I looked at each other and probably would have made some sort of comment, but a nurse appeared, telling us that Laura was coming to.

Laura

I was trapped in a tunnel with no exit, while a force was wrenching me from my insides. I couldn't fight it. There was no strength to do so. But then I was floating on the waves of the ocean, a rhythmic beep lulling me—until an unbearable pain assaulted me once more. I begged it to stop, then wondered if that's what death felt like. There was a flurry of white, the rush of footsteps, and beaming lights blazing around me. The demands to push.

There was no urge to push. No urge to do anything but sleep. But sleep did not come. Then there was the distant sound of mewing.

"It's a girl! Laura. Laura?"

My work was done. Darkness slipped over the bright lights and I swirled away, whirling inward. Like rust-colored water gurgling down the shower drain.

The few times I opened my eyes, I saw Eric and Jenny's faces and I wanted to ask about the baby. I was certain I had her, but I couldn't lift my arms to touch my belly for confirmation. Then I would sink into darkness again. It seems I do this frequently, unwillingly. Voices, blips, and the shuffling of bodies would stir me out of oblivion; sometimes the words make sense, other times I only wish for silence.

"Laura? Can you hear me? Squeeze my hand if you can hear me."

I try to say I can hear him, but I have little strength to do so.

"Laura?" Dr. Kim's face comes into view. I must have opened my eyes. "Hello there."

My sights shifted from his face to the mass of tubes attached to me.

"You have a little girl."

That's when I gasped for air. I needed to see her.

"How long," I began, but my mouth was too dry to speak. A moist cloth was brought to my lips and I sucked on it. Then I said, "She okay?"

"She's fine. Five pounds, four ounces. You had her two days ago."

I choked up. "Need to see her."

"You will. You're still very weak."

"When?" The thought of my daughter not knowing who I was awakened my senses. "I need to see her."

Dr. Kim patted my hand. "I'll see what I can do, but you have some very anxious people waiting outside." He walked out of the room and I began to feel a sense of panic. I needed to see my baby.

"Hey," Eric said, walking into the room. He came up to my bed and dusted my cheek with a kiss. Jenny stood next to him. Their eyes were red-rimmed, their clothes disheveled.

"I did it," I muttered.

"Yes, you did," Jenny said. "She's so precious."

"You saw her?"

"Just through the nursery window and it wasn't for long."

"I need to see her," I said.

"You're so weak, sis," Eric said.

He was right and I couldn't keep my eyes opened any longer in spite of how I tried to fight it.

When I opened my eyes again, Eric and Jenny were nowhere in sight. The room was quiet, but I had a newfound strength. Maggie appeared.

"Well, look who's awake!"

I gave her a weak smile.

"You gave us quite a scare, lass."

"Didn't think I was going to make it, did you?" I said.

"Oh, merciful Jesus, I never said that. You're a fighter, you are." She came over and brushed the hair from my face.

"Maggie, I want to see my baby."

"They haven't brought her to you, yet?"

Tears began to stream down my face.

"Oh, there, there. We can't have none of that." She pulled some tissues from the box on the stand next to the bed and dabbed at my face. "I have other patients needin' me, but I'll see what I can do."

I didn't doubt her and a short time later she appeared back in the room, but this time carrying a tiny bundle. I tried to sit up, but she told me to stay still. With one hand, she moved the tubes aside and then placed my daughter on my chest without really letting go.

"Is she breathing," I said, my heart pounding.

"Yes, lass. She's just asleep."

I stared at her, at the wonder of her. What would Peter make of her?

"She's lackin' something, wouldn't you say?"

"No!" I said, annoyed with the implication. "She's perfect."

"That what you're callin' her? She? She's lackin' a name, wouldn't you say?"

"Oh," I said, gazing down at the way her lips looked to be shaped in a perfect kiss. "I do have a name. I picked it out months ago."

"Well, don't keep me wonderin'."

"Anastasia Desirée."

"That's certainly a mouthful for such a tiny one, no?"

"Anastasia means, the resurrection of springtime."

"That's rather perfect then, and what about Desirée?

"Longed for."

"Ahh. That she was."

I'd fallen asleep with the memory of Anastasia. The next morning I woke eager to see her again. Instead, Dr. Kim came in. He told me I was too weak for chemo, too weak to be able to fight what I had. He stayed with me, holding my hand, trying to provide lay terms for my hopeless condition.

"You need to make some decisions for your daughter," he said. "It wouldn't be fair of me to give false hope when that baby's future depends on you."

Eric and Jenny appeared just as Dr. Kim was leaving the room. They came over and each gave me a kiss on the forehead. Crying had exhausted me, but I couldn't sleep. Not until I spoke to Eric and Jenny.

"I got to hold her," I said. "Last night."

"Oh," Jenny said. "I'm so glad."

"I guess I should tell you her name." And when I did they both repeated it with a note of uncertainty.

I closed my eyes, wishing to never have to say what needed to be said. "I have to…" My throat closed up and Eric rested his hand on my arm. I opened my eyes and started again. "I have to talk to the two of you about something."

Jenny immediately took the chair at the foot of the bed, but Eric remained standing.

"Dr. Kim was just in here," I said, taking a deep breath, unsure how to proceed. "He told me what you probably already know."

Eric's chin began to quiver.

"Your prayers were answered," I said.

He scowled. "What did Dr. Kim say?"

"I can't keep my baby." The statement came out hoarse.

"Not now," Eric said, "but you're going to fight this."

"How, Eric?"

Eric leaned down in my face. "With every ounce of your strength. You're going to beat this."

I gazed into his tear-filled eyes. "You really believe that?"

"I have to," he said.

"The doctor told you otherwise, didn't he?"

"I don't care what he says."

"You don't see it, do you?" I said.

"What?"

"I was never the one running this show."

"I don't understand," Eric said.

In a whisper, I said, "She was never meant to be mine."

"No," Eric said. "No. She's what you're going to be fighting for."

"Dr. Kim says it's too late," I said.

"Dr. Kim doesn't have faith," Eric said.

"I'm tired of fighting Him, Eric"

"You don't have to; we'll get you a new doctor."

"No, not the doctor. Him."

From the foot of the bed, Jenny blurted, "You mean God."

"The best I can hope for is that she's going to get the love she deserves."

"What are you saying?" Jenny said, standing.

"She's yours," I sputtered. "God used me to give her to you."

Eric stared at me. "No! That's ridiculous."

Jenny was shaking, tears streaming down her face.

"Why, Eric? Are you saying God doesn't work that way?"

"I'm saying you've got to get better! You're giving up."

"Don't give up, Laura," Jenny said, her voice shaky.

"Please, just tell me you'll take her, so I can at least know...."

"Of course, we'll take care of her," Eric said, "until you get better." He reached down and hugged me.

CHAPTER TWENTY

Laura

There is no talk of tomorrows anymore. Whenever a doctor or nurse comes in the room, they ask if I'm comfortable. I nod and tell them yes. It's not the truth, but I think they like to hear it. Comfort seems to be the objective. I wait for the couple of hours each day when they bring Anastasia to me. That's when I forget the pain and feel a fight in me that believes a miracle may keep me alive for my daughter. I don't hold her much, but they put the cart in the space next to my bed and let me look at her, which is all I do. When she's not here, I tug the strings of the pink helium-filled balloons announcing, *It's A Girl!* and bob them along the ceiling.

Or I sleep. I sleep a lot. That's what I was doing when I was awakened by a presence. I opened my eyes to see Peter standing in the doorway. Peter. He came over to me with some hesitation. I stared at him, unable to stop the tears. When I could finally speak, I asked how he found me.

"Loren. Apparently, your brother told him. He didn't waste a moment and rang me. I've been back in London." He paused. "Wasn't sure how you'd feel about me coming here."

"Everything I tried to do seems so silly now," I said. "I'm just sorry you came all this way. Loren shouldn't have bothered you."

"Actually, he saved me from drowning in self-pity."

I reached over and took his hand. "It's a girl."

"I know."

"She's so beautiful, Peter."

"Of course, she is," he said, running his hand through my hair. "Look who her mummy is."

There was a shuffling of feet at the door. I looked across the room to see Jenny standing in the doorway.

"Jenny," I said, "Peter's here. Remember Pe--"

"I remember. Just what are you doing here?"

Eric

Just when I thought things couldn't get any worse, I now have a wife who's out of control. "Why don't you just wait and see?" I said.

Jenny responded by taking a pillow from the couch and flinging it at me before storming off to the kitchen.

"He was there!" Jenny said. "Doesn't that scare you?"

"Scare me? No, Jenny. Laura needed to see him. Loren knew that."

"You had to go and say something!" She knocked a chair onto the floor. I could hardly believe this irate woman was Jenny.

I placed the chair back at the table. "Why don't we just trust the Lord—"

"Trust the Lord? Trust the Lord? And while we're going through all this trusting, this man takes our baby away from us?" She shoved the chair again. "No, Eric, it's not going to happen. We need a legal document stating she wants us to be the parents!"

"How can I ask her to do that?" Eric said. "It'll mean ... it'll mean I don't believe she's going to survive...."

"She's accepted what's happening. I think you need to, too. Otherwise, we're going to lose this chance."

It was almost one in the morning. The long battle exhausted me. Without another word, I went out the door. I never walked out on Jenny before, but I couldn't stop myself. I broke into a sprint, but as I got further away, I slowed back to a stride. A full moon drenched the sidewalk's path while Seabrook slept. Overhead, towering ancient oaks were beginning to bud. It wasn't officially spring yet, but the air was warm. My steady pace carried me and my thoughts and soon I found myself in front of the Sumner house, the stagnant For Sale sign planted on the front lawn.

The house was dark and I imagined that Beth was asleep. I wondered how she could with so much bitterness stewing inside of her. I called to let her know she should make her peace with our sister, but was met with silence.

"Beth?"

"What do you want me to say?"

"Something compassionate, something sisterly, would be nice." Then I hung up.

I looked up to the star-filled heavens. Could Laura be right that this was some master plan over which she had little control, in spite of all her arranging? If so, that was not how I wanted a baby. To shake my fist at those heavens would have felt right.

I turned and began to run until I was close enough to the parsonage to see Jenny standing on the sidewalk. She started toward me and when we met, she wrapped her arms tight around my neck and begged my forgiveness.

"I said some awful things," she said through her tears.

I forgave her before she was even in my arms. But to be honest, I wondered where this Peter Collins fits in all this myself. How can you deny a father his child? I know the answer to that. But how will we, Jenny and I, survive the loss?

The next day, I was in the quiet of the sanctuary on my knees, praying for God to help me with the questions.

"Parson Sumner?"

I got up and turned, facing the back of the sanctuary. "Why don't you call me Eric," I said, slipping my hands in my pockets.

"And you can call me Peter." He cleared his throat. "I've come to talk to you about—"

Neither of us made a move toward the other.

"I know why you're here, Mr. Collins."

Laura

I am lulled by the gentle tapping of Peter's typewriter and the barely perceptible sound of Anastasia's breathing. I lay on my side, my baby in the crook of my arm. For the time being, we are a family. Anastasia could have been discharged days ago, but Peter suggested she be set up in my room, with him promising to be available to change her diaper and feed her.

"I can't be there for her like your brother and sister can, but for now, I think she should be with you."

The hospital staff went along with his suggestion and it was Maggie who believed it was Anastasia who gave me a reason not to give up. She was right. There are some moments when I question whether or not I'm really dying. I feel too alive to be doing so. But I know that my baby girl will be going home with Eric and Jenny when the time comes, their fears having been put to rest. In my heart, I hope the time never comes. In my mind, I know it will. In Peter's romance novel, the one that he reads me in the quiet of the evening, I not only survive, but end up having it all. Oh, the wonder of fiction.

So now my days are filled with what can only be described as sorrowful contentment. If I think about what Anastasia will look like in a few years or how her voice will sound, I slip into unspeakable grief. For now, I gaze down on her and watch as she stares back at me. I want her to always remember this moment.

But the spell is broken when a nurse comes in and pops a thermometer in my mouth. Peter stops typing and scoops the baby up and bops her on his shoulder.

"Soon you'll be knocking down a few walls and putting up a mailbox," the nurse said. She was laughing at her joke until she pulled the thermometer from my mouth.

"Nurse?" Peter said.

I saw her look of concern, too. She motioned for him to follow her outside of the room. He placed the baby in the bassinet next to me. A few minutes later, he wandered back in, rubbing the stubble on his face. I had to ask twice what was wrong before he replied.

"Can't get your fever down."

That was not news. Even after trying one antibiotic after the next, I had a fever that would not go away.

"Listen, she's asleep now," he said, glancing in the crib. "I'd like to see if I can find the doctor."

"It's gone up, hasn't it?"

"Probably too much activity. You need your rest." He pulled the covers up to my chin.

"Please don't let them take her yet," I said.

"I won't."

"Will you be long?"

He kissed my forehead. "No."

"Thank you," I said.

He caressed my cheek. "Get some sleep."

After he left, I tried to sleep, but my eyes were locked on Anastasia, her tiny form so still I worried she wasn't breathing. I was about to call for help when I finally saw the faint rise and fall of her chest.

"Laura?"

I looked up to see Beth standing in the doorway.

"You awake?" She took a step further in.

I nodded.

Anastasia let out a whimper. Beth barely glanced at her.

In a whisper, I said, "Isn't she beautiful?"

"Eric tells me you're giving her to them."

The whimpering started to build. I forced myself up to a sitting position, my body shaking. "Would you please hand her to me?"

She backed away, her eyes wide. "You mean, pick her up?"

"Beth, please. She's crying."

Anastasia began to wail, and Beth went over and reached in. She started to pick her up, but then jumped back, leaving my daughter to scream.

"No, this is wrong. It's wrong that you had her, that you purposely—"

Sheer will power moved me out of bed, my feet landing on the floor. With the IV dragging alongside of me, I went to the bassinet. Every part of me trembled as I leaned over and picked her up. *Please don't let me drop her.*

"Make her stop crying!" Beth said, covering her ears.

I rested her against my shoulder and patted her back, soothing her to silence. My legs buckled just as I reached my bed. I landed on the mattress and situated myself, collapsing against the pillows. When I looked up, tears were streaming down Beth's face.

"Why do you get to keep her?" she said. "Why is it okay for you and not me?"

I tried to make sense of her words. "What?" I said.

"Sixteen was not too young to know what I wanted. He said he loved me."

"Who, Beth?"

"But then when he found out I was going to have his baby…"

My heart began to pound. "You're talking about Pastor Allen."

"He said I had to give it up."

"Oh, Beth." I wanted to get up and wrap my arms around her, but had no strength left to do so. "How could I not know this?"

"Because he sent me off to Kansas," she said.

"Kansas? When you were at the retreat?"

"There was no retreat! He had me stay with a cousin of his, a nasty lady who told me I was evil."

That sonofabitch.

"I thought we were going to be a family," she said.

"Did Mom—"

"She didn't know."

"Beth, you didn't do anything wrong. He was the evil one."

"No. It was my fault. I tempted him. He told me I was a Jezebel."

"He was wrong, Beth. You were just a child."

She straightened up, brushed the tears away. "All I know is that God punishes the wicked."

"I don't believe you were wicked, Beth."

"Of course I was, and so are you."

"No, we're not."

"I had to give it up. I don't even know if it was a boy or a girl." She looked over at Anastasia resting in my arms.

I was shaking uncontrollably and wasn't sure if it was from Beth's revelation or the fever. "You need help, Beth. You need—"

"It's okay, because God is just. You don't get to keep your baby either. He saw to that!" Then, without another word, she tore out of the room. I called to her but she was gone.

I was too stunned to cry while trying to digest the news. Where was Peter? I needed him to calm me down. I gazed at my daughter in the curve of my arm. For some unexplainable reason, I opened my hospital gown and offered Anastasia my breast. She wriggled and cooed, having little idea what to do with it. There was no nourishment to offer so I covered myself back up and curled a tuft of her downy-like hair around my finger, imagining what it would have been like to be her mother. With my daughter stretching and twitching next to me, I envisioned all of her firsts—her first word, her first steps, her first Easter egg hunt, searching for pastel-colored eggs—and closed my eyes.

CHAPTER TWENTY-ONE

Eric

When Peter called to tell me that Laura had slipped into a coma, I had a zillion questions for him but was unable to formulate a single one. Peter did say that he'd gone to find a doctor and by the time he returned he found Anastasia wailing next to Laura. That's when he realized something had to be terribly wrong when the screaming didn't wake Laura.

That had been two days ago. I guess. It's hard to tell how much time passed when you're keeping vigil. But I'm not alone. Peter stays by the bedside holding Laura's hand and Jenny is here, too, the rhythmic beep of the monitor keeping us company. Jenny holds her gaze on a dried-up flower arrangement, a pencil in her hand and a sketch pad on her lap. The last time I wandered by her, the page was blank. We took turns calling the house to ask Jenny's parents how the baby was doing. I told Dr. Kim that perhaps we should keep Anastasia nearby, in case Laura wakes and is looking for her. Dr. Kim said he did not believe that was any longer a possibility.

"What do you mean?" I said. "You don't think she's going to come out of this?"

"I'd be very surprised."

"Then you don't know how our Lord works," I said.

He put his hand on my shoulder and said, "I think I do."

I had called Beth, but there was no answer. Don told me he'd keep trying until he got a hold of her.

A pink balloon, the helium drained from it, skittered across the floor. Dr. Kim came in and was going through the routine of listening to my sister's heartbeat. He pulled the stethoscope from his ears.

"She's so weak," he said, standing over the bed, gazing down at her. He started to say something else, but then simply walked out.

Peter returned to his spot and lifted Laura's hand, then rested his head on the bed and closed his eyes. Jenny was slumped on her chair, snoring lightly. I, too, found it to be a battle to stay awake. *Make your face shine upon us, Lord. Give us a miracle*, I prayed, and then closed my eyes.

Laura

There we were, the three of us, except that Anastasia is older. No one told me it was Anastasia, but I just knew. Her hair billowed out from her shoulders as she whirled in the circle, holding hands with Peter and me. Her voice was melodious, as she sang, "Ring around the rosy, a pocket full of posies, ashes, ashes...."

And we all fell down on the lush green grass, laughing, until I heard my name being called. I turned to see a man in the distance, on top of a hill.

"Laura."

"Come on, Mommy. Again. Ring around the rosy...."

"Laura!"

This time I recognized the voice. "Dad?" He came a bit closer, the whole hill seemingly coming closer. Yes, Dad! He waved at me, signaling for me to go to him.

"Ashes, ashes...."

But I didn't fall down. Instead, I let go of Peter and Anastasia's hands and started toward the hill. "Come, come meet my father!" I called back to them.

"Laura!" Peter shouted, but I kept running, refusing to look back, drawing closer and closer, clambering up the hill.

Eric

Stop that damn shrieking! I struggled to open my eyes. How long had I been sleeping? In a blur, I saw Jenny standing over the bed, her shoulders shaking. In front of her, Peter hovered over Laura, calling her.

Then I saw the monitor. There were no more bleeps. No wavy bumps traveling across the screen. Only a horrifying horizontal line.

And that awful shriek.

I told myself to run, go get help, but I was transfixed. Then a mass of white appeared, blocking my view, a confusion of voices shouting orders.

Finally, the shrieking stopped.

The voices silenced.

The mass of white dispersed.

"11:35 p.m.," Dr. Kim said, rubbing his eyes. I stood at the foot of the bed, staring through watery eyes. Jenny fell into me. Peter remained huddled over Laura.

"I have to see the baby," Jenny said. "I need to hold her."

I knew what she meant. Peter must have, too, because he looked up, his eyes red, and asked if he could come as well.

Still, none of us moved, the three of us watching, perhaps hoping she'd suddenly come up gasping, as if almost having drowned, but suddenly conquering death.

It would have been a miracle I could have accepted.

CHAPTER TWENTY-TWO

Beth

The sun was so bright it glistened off Laura's casket. Eric struggled to compose himself. Finally, he said, "This was one of my sister's favorite passages," and began to read from Psalms. As if Laura ever read the Bible!

From where I was sitting, I could see Jenny cradling that baby, the prize possession. She and Eric sold their souls to get her. Must have. Mother always said that people who take their eyes off the Lord make deals with the devil.

Eric finished reading and closed his Bible. His legs buckled and Don started toward him, but the Englishman reached him first and steadied him. Then everyone took turns tossing flowers on the coffin before heading back to their cars. And that was that. It was over. I watched Jenny keeping the baby near to her as she navigated the cemetery with the Englishman as her guide. Eric hadn't budged from the coffin next to the gaping hole and pile of dirt.

"Beth?" Don said, coming up to me and touching me on the shoulder. "How you doing?"

"A lot better than my brother. Hard to think of him as pastor of this church with the way he's going on. He's supposed to be stronger than that."

"I guess he realizes what he lost today. She was a wonderful, bright woman."

"Eric acts like she was a saint."

There was that look again, this time from Don. Eric and Jenny have been giving me that same appalled look for weeks now, as if Laura shouldn't pay for her sins; as if I were the one who refused to listen to my mother and Pastor Allen. I *always* listened. Still do.

"You need a ride?" Don said.

I shook my head. "Mary's offered to drive me." Might be plain foolish to ride with a deaf woman, but at least she doesn't make me feel funny the way Don does. I left him standing there and went over to see how Eric was doing. I found him alone by the casket. He turned to face me, his shoulders slumped, his eyes strained.

I said, "You're taking this pretty hard."

He didn't say anything, just shook his head and looked up toward the heavens.

"It's time," I said, "you get back to the Lord, reclaim your faith."

"*Reclaim* my faith?"

"All this talk about unconditional love—"

He crouched down and began scratching his finger in the dirt next to the grave.

"What are you doing?" I waited, but he said nothing, he just kept scrawling. "Eric, I'm speaking to you. What are you doing?"

He looked up at me, squinting. "Remember that story from John where the scribes and Pharisees bring the adulteress before Jesus?"

I scuffed my feet, unsure where this was going. However, I blurted, "John: 8, 7."

"Right. Do you recall what Jesus was doing when they brought her to him?"

"Of course." This was silly, but then I faltered to see him hunkered on the ground. "He was, well, he was writing something in the sand."

He nodded. "But do you remember what he wrote?"

"It was never revealed what he actually wrote, Eric. I'm surprised you forgot—"

"That's true," he said, standing. He was rolling pebbles in the palm of his hand and he didn't seem to be as shaky as he had been. "It doesn't say. And maybe it's not supposed to. Maybe Jesus was purposely being slow to judge."

"Is there a point to all this?"

He closed his eyes and looked to be thinking. "I know you believe Mom was wonderful, Beth. I know you think she was the example you should follow, but she wasn't."

"I don't have to hear this." I turned to walk away, but he grabbed me by the arm.

"What Mom did to us was wrong."

"Don't say that!" I struggled to free myself, but he wouldn't let go. "You're hurting me."

"Hurting? No, Beth. Belts, sticks, hairbrushes. They hurt."

"She was doing what Pastor told her to do—"

"Pastor Allen was an evil man, Beth."

My scream was shrill: "Don't say that!"

He pressed the pebbles into my hand. "Here, this is pretty much what you've wanted to do all these years. It should be easier now that she's no longer a moving target."

I broke free, letting the pebbles fall from my hand. I heard Don call me, but I kept going until I reached Mary, who was waiting for me in her car. I asked her to take me home and once we got there, I discouraged her from coming in. Maybe I should have let her come in because the voices were persistent. I ran upstairs, but no matter what room I went to they followed.

What a good girl you are. My sweet Beth.

I ran back downstairs, into the kitchen, the kitchen of yesteryear. Mom is standing at the counter, preparing dinner.

Pastor says you're his favorite.

"He loves me, Mom!"

Let's take these off, Beth.

I can't. Please, no. I don't want him to see me naked, but he insists I should obey. He always relies upon the verse: *obey them that have rule over you, and submit yourselves. You must submit yourself, Beth, if you love me.*

I dash back into the living room, repeating the verse until I remember that there is more to it. For they watch for your souls, as they must give account. "They must give account!" I screamed, running and bumping into the spider plant. But she is now standing next to it.

Look at all these shoots, Beth. It's flourishing, because it's rooted in the right things. And you wouldn't have won those if you weren't rooted in the right things. She points to the trophies on the shelf across the room.

A shoot from the plant grazed my arm and I grabbed it, snapping it off. It felt nothing but good, so I pulled the whole plant from the hanging rope. She screamed for me to stop, quoting verses to make me do so, but I was determined to go on. The ceramic pot was heavy, but I lifted it as high as I could and—damn the voices warning me to stop—I hurled it, targeting the line of trophies.

But it crashed only a short distance from my feet.

I dropped to me knees, scrambling in the dirt and ceramic shards. "They must give account! They must give account!" I crushed the mass of roots with the heels of my hands, trying to destroy them all, making certain there'll never be another offshoot.

Suddenly, I felt myself being lifted, levitated from the dirt. I kicked and screamed, expecting to see him. If anyone could rise from the dead it would have been Pastor Allen.

"It's all right, Beth! It's all right. It's just me. Don."

I was steered toward the couch and guided to sit down. He pulled me into him. I was too weak and shaky to push away. "Don? It's you?" I said, my voice quivering.

"Yes, it's me, sweetheart."

While I began to sob, quietly at first, but then uncontrollably, he kept telling me I'd be all right. His voice began to calm me until my cries had diminished. I rested against the barrel of his chest and heard the rhythmic sound of the clock on the end table. I hadn't heard the ticking cadence in ages and realized it was no longer competing with the voices.

Eventually, I said, "What's happening to me?"

"Looks to me like you're sorting through things." He dabbed the blood on my hands and knees with his handkerchief.

I looked at the crushed plant and broken ceramic pot. For as long as I recall it hung in the picture window. It stunned me what I'd done, what I'd been able to do; how still the room was, except for the perceptible passing of time.

"Laura's gone," I said. It was a statement, but for the first time I tried to make sense of the weight of it.

"Yes, yes she is."

I was numb with grief and despair. How was I supposed to go on without her? "I'll miss her so much," I whispered.

"So will a lot of people."

"Look what I've done." I pointed to the mess on the floor.

"Nothing a broom and dustpan can't handle. The other stuff, well that can't be swept away so easy."

"Laura was right. I need help, Don." Saying it made me feel stronger. "I was so awful to her."

"You were," he said. "You were pretty awful to a lot of people."

I looked up into his brown eyes.

"But you didn't mean to be," he said. "There's still time for you to change all that."

At first I couldn't imagine how that would be possible. Laura was gone. But then minutes turned into an hour and even though I didn't think I could move, it became clear what I needed to do.

"Why don't we begin with me taking you over to Eric and Jenny's?" Don said. You all need to grieve together."

"The baby," I said.

"She's going to be a part of your life, Beth."

I trembled at the thought, then it slowly dawned on me that I needed to accept that child. In a whisper and tentatively, I said, "I think I'd like to see Annelise."

"Anastasia. Her name is Anastasia."

I considered it. Leave it to Laura to pick a name like that. "Anastasia," I said aloud. "I don't believe I know any Anastasias."

Don smiled and hugged me. "You do now."

EPILOGUE

Jenny

I tossed a sheet over the canvas and shifted the easel into the corner. The painting is a surprise for Eric's birthday, and I can't wait to see his expression when I give it to him. A gentle breeze lured me to the open window. I leaned on the sill, gazing up at the hundreds of stars. I breathed in the warm spring air, searching for the brightest star, imagining it was the twinkle in Laura's eye. After all, her daughter turned a year old today.

What a treat to hold the birthday party in our big Victorian house, the one we bought a few months ago. We may not have furnished and decorated it elegantly enough for a *House Beautiful* spread, but it's home. Everyone we invited came, far more than we could have crammed into the living room of the parsonage. Eric convinced the board to use the parsonage to put up visiting missionaries or families who were temporarily homeless for one reason or another. I love him for thinking like that.

He's also the one who remembered to invite Loren and Esther. Moments after they arrived, they sprawled on the floor with the birthday girl to help her open their present—a rocking horse! Of course, she can't ride it by herself yet, but Loren and Esther on either side keeping her steady as they rocked her is a wonderful shot for the memory book I'm making. Another shot caught Anastasia smearing frosting on her Aunt Beth and Uncle Don's faces. I hope I captured the look on Beth's face; her smile any wider and her face would have disappeared. She's become a new woman.

Funny, too, watching Beth and Don bat the dozens of balloons back and forth to each other, behaving as newlyweds should. The other day Beth actually turned poetic, telling me how Don mended the hem of her unraveled life and each day adds a new stitch of love to keep her secure. Imagine Beth saying something as syrupy as that. Bringing her from her old to her new self took all the therapy in creation, and she's still not done, but she's come so far. I mean, there's a lot to say for therapy, and Beth is a living testament. "A good old fashioned sermon does my heart good," she said to Eric last Sunday, "but I really look forward to my weekly appointments."

Later that night, after Anastasia was sound asleep and Eric and I were in bed, Eric said, "I'll be."

"What?" I said, barely keeping my eyes opened.

"That night, the night Laura died, I prayed for a miracle."

"And?"

"I got it. It wasn't the one I was asking for, but with the change in Beth, I got one."

The change in Beth meant that we were free to put the house back on the market. It didn't take long to sell it, either. It was only a couple of months later, when Don sold his, as well. Now, Beth and Don live in the condo they bought a few blocks away. They have a spare bedroom that they are fixing up for Anastasia when she stays overnight. That's fine with me, since Eric and I look forward to an occasional night for ourselves.

I recalled the faces surrounding Anastasia when I placed the cake with the single candle in front of her. From grandparents to friends, everyone sang "Happy Birthday," including her father. That's how we designate Peter, who is Anastasia's father. Eric is Daddy. Daddy comes home every night, but Father only on special occasions; like birthday parties, for instance. Peter doesn't know what to make of her and I can tell he's in awe. His visits are becoming less and less, but each time he's about to leave, he thanks us for loving her so well.

I took one more long breath of air, then lifted the sheet from the canvas to give it another look. I guess I do have artistic talent, especially when it comes to painting children's likenesses. There was Anastasia smiling, holding her soon-to-be brother's hand. I reproduced the three by five Polaroid that Beginnings gave us of our baby waiting to come from Vietnam. He was about a month old when the photo was taken and we have about another month before he arrives. Eric and I are beside ourselves with worry since there's so much unrest over there. Soon, though, we'll be driving to the airport to pick up Samuel Jason. Samuel means "asked of God." Beth told me Jason means "healer," which is why we chose that as his middle name. Eric is hoping to have a child from every continent filling up this drafty old house. Now, my getting pregnant doesn't seem so important.

I toss the sheet back over the painting and skip to the floor below and down the hallway. I hear Eric's voice coming from the nursery. I stop in the doorway to watch. In the rocking chair, in her daddy's arms, is Anastasia sprawled out, her eyes closed and mouth lax. But that doesn't stop Eric from his nightly routine of reading to her. This time I hear he chose a personal favorite. The book is open on his lap, but his gaze is fixed on the stuffed pink goose on the toy chest.

> "So, let me advise you and say it loud
> It's great being an original in a very common crowd
> Just as Goose first regretted being pink
> She'll warn you profusely to stop and think
> Don't go seeking to find what's not there
> For you are you, wonderful and rare."

He kissed her on the forehead, then walked over and placed her into her crib. I tiptoed in and wrapped my arms around his waist. We stand for a few minutes watching her sleep in perfect peace, until I say, "Come on, honey, let's go to bed."

AUTHOR'S NOTE

It was 1989 when I began writing *Of Little Faith*, which first started as a memoir. I had just begun to pull away from a fundamental Bible-believing church that I had been a member of for several years and needed to sort out what I was going through. I began to see contradictions, not only in members of this church, but in the very book on which we based our beliefs. Initially, I struggled with the doubts and questions I was having, believing they were inspired by the devil. After all, the church I attended had warned its congregation that, according to the Bible, the devil had ways of making us doubt our faith and tricking us, but it was that same Bible that taught us that we would not be tested beyond what we could bear (1 Corinthians 10:13). However, I couldn't help but think about the fifteen year-old active member of our church who must have been tested beyond what he could bear since he went home one afternoon and took his father's pistol, loaded it and put it in his mouth, pulling the trigger. He left a message telling his family to look at it as if he had never been born; fifteen years old and he felt he had no way out except to kill himself.

Even though I wasn't close to this family, that boy's pain haunted me for years; still does. Something wasn't meeting his needs, even though we sang hymns about Jesus walking and talking with us and being our comfort. Naturally, there were certain people in the congregation who gave excuses about why this boy did what he did, how he wasn't relying on God; how the devil had his way.

Then there were the weekly Bible studies I attended faithfully, the ones where we were studying the book of Job. Finally, as we were wrapping up that particular book, the pastor, who was leading the study, reminded us of how Job never really knew why he lost his children, riches and good health, but he was blessed with more children, got back his riches and was healed—and most importantly, never cursed God. Murmurs around the room muttered, "Praise Jesus."

Praise Jesus?

Hesitantly, I spoke up. "Well, Job doesn't know, but we're told why. Satan approached God and used Job as the chess piece. I'm not comfortable with that. I want a God who will protect me from such challenges."

After there was an uncomfortable silence, one woman in the group said, "But he was blessed after that!"

I turned and asked her if her children died would having more children replace them? She blanched and shut her mouth.

I think that may have been the last time I attended the Bible study and my attendance at church began to dwindle. That is not to say my decision was callous. No, I often found myself curled up on my couch sobbing, afraid I'd be going to hell because my faith did not hold up to my questions. The pastor made a last ditch effort to get me to come back to church, but when I explained to him my reasoning as to why I was having doubts, he admitted that most believers didn't entertain the thoughts that I was having because it was just too much to consider. So, I started to write about it and thought maybe a memoir would sort it out for me. However, two weeks into the process, I realized that no one was going to care about this thirty-something year old who was wrestling with her own demons. Then, suddenly, a voice announced, "I never meant to hurt anyone."

This wasn't an actual voice, mind you, but one in my head, one that belonged to a young woman who became Laura Sumner. I just had to figure out what she meant and before long she was battling her siblings and her mother's God from the tips of my fingers to the keys of my electric typewriter. That's when my memoir became a work of fiction.

But, if I were to be honest, I knew the character of Beth uncomfortably well. When I was in the throes of my church, I believed as Beth believed. I took the Bible at its word. I'm sure my family, who was not a part of this church, found me to be obnoxious and myopic. And, there was also a part of me in Jenny, the part who wanted children. I did give birth to my son a year and a half after I married, but then several years later when it appeared that I'd never get pregnant again, I adopted my two daughters from Korea, which was something I'd always wanted to do, anyway. Therefore, I wasn't as panicked as Jenny, but I could relate to her frustration.

Of Little Faith is not my first published novel, but it is the first novel I wrote. I would live and breathe these characters all hours of the day and night and the story unfolded rather easily. Actually, it was written in six weeks. Okay, the first draft was written in six weeks. It then went through many, many more drafts for as many years until I was as satisfied as I could be. Well, I'm sure I would still want to tweak this or that, but there comes a time when one must let it go and move on, which is basically what I did with that fundamental church.

People sometimes ask me what my beliefs are now. It's more what those beliefs aren't. I am no longer the arrogant young woman I had been who was so sure she had all the answers, thanks to the hefty book she referenced day and night. I no longer believe that the Bible is infallible. What do I believe in now? Well, for one, I believe it is okay to ask the tough questions, even if one's faith cannot stand up to them. But, more importantly, I believe that compassion cures more "sins" than condemnation.

JUN 2014

CPSIA information can be obtained at www.ICGtesting.com
Printed in the USA
BVOW08s1554170614

356622BV00009B/109/P